WHERE WILL WE SPEND ETERNITY?

The Location and Inhabitants of Heaven and Hell Over Time

DR. CARLTON L. BURFORD

ISBN 978-1-964462-82-0 (Paperback)
ISBN 978-1-964462-83-7 (Ebook)

Inquiries and Book Orders should be addressed to:

Leavitt Peak Press
17901 Pioneer Blvd Ste L #298, Artesia, California 90701
Phone #: 2092191548

Acknowledgments

I would like to thank my wife, Bernetta L. Burford, for her unwavering support in the writing of this book. Her support was very much needed in this project.

I would also like to thank all those who provided me feedback and input on the initial manuscript of this book.

May God richly bless you all.

Contents

Chapter 1

Introduction

After forty-three years of ministry, including preaching, teaching, and counseling, I have engaged with many on the topics of heaven, hell, and the afterlife. Some believed in heaven but not hell, some believed in annihilation after death, and some believed that as soon as they died, they would be walking in heaven on streets of gold. However, hardly anyone talked about how things were initially created and how they, and their occupants, would change over time.

I am writing this book with the purpose and hope of providing light and biblical proof of how things began and how they have indeed changed over time. All in the master plan of the Almighty God. Let's get started.

Chapter 2

The Beginning

In the beginning, God created the heavens and the earth. During the six days of creation, God created the atmosphere around the earth (heaven), light, dry land, vegetation, the sun and moon, marine life, winged fowl, and land animals, and finally, for the pinnacle of His creation, God made man. After the six days of creation, God ceased His creative works. Everything was now in place for history to unfold itself.

In reference to Jesus and the creation, Colossians 1:16 says, **"For by him were all things created, that are in heaven, and that are in earth, visible and invisible, whether they be thrones, or dominions, or principalities, or powers: all things were created by him, and for him"** (KJV).

Everything necessary for man's existence for life and death was in place, including the angels. Hebrews 1:13–14 says, **"But to which of the angels said he at any time, Sit on my right hand, until I make thine enemies thy footstool?**

"14 Are they not all ministering spirits, sent forth to minister for them who shall be heirs of salvation?" (KJV).

Not only do angels worship and minister to God, but also they minister to those who are heirs of salvation—the redeemed.

Since God is omniscient (knows all things), included in the creation were also the temporary and final places of departed souls/spirits of people who would die, the prisons of the fallen angels who sinned by taking human wives and having children by them, the Abyss, and the Lake of Fire.

Though we tend to speak of two places the departed souls/spirits go after death (heaven and hell), this is done to simplify things in our minds. The Bible has many references to the places of the dead, including *Sheol*, the grave, paradise, *Hades*, heaven, and a special place for some of the fallen angels who sinned—*Tartaros*.

I will mention here that *Sheol* and *Hades* refer to the same place. *Sheol* is the Hebrew word, and *Hades* is the Greek equivalent of the English word "hell." Before the resurrection of Jesus, "Paradise" was part of *Sheol/Hades*. I will show that after the resurrection of Jesus, the paradise side of *Sheol/Hades* was translated to the third heaven.

Finally, there is the Lake of Fire and Brimstone, also known by the Greek word *Gehenna*, which is the final and permanent dwelling place of all unsaved people and all the fallen angels, including Satan.

I will also show in this book how the occupants of these locations have changed over time.

In the next chapter, let's define the locations of the departed souls/spirits as noted above.

Chapter 3

Definitions

1) The Grave – the place where the physical body is deposited after death (the separation of the soul/spirit from the body). This place has remained the same from before the resurrection of Jesus until after the resurrection.

Genesis 35:20

And Jacob set a pillar upon her **grave**: that is the pillar of Rachel's **grave** unto this day.

(KJV)

2) Sheol – the Hebrew word for the place of all the departed souls/spirits before the resurrection of Jesus from the grave. After the resurrection of Jesus, the occupants of Sheol changed as we will see later. *Sheol* is translated in English as "hell."

Jonah 2:2

And said, I cried by reason of mine affliction unto the Lord, and he heard me; out of the belly of hell (*Sheol*) cried I, and thou heardest my voice.

(KJV)

3) Hades – This is the same place as Sheol above and is the Greek equivalent.

4) Paradise – This was the comfort side of Sheol/Hades, also known as Abraham's bosom before the resurrection of Jesus, but its location was changed after His resurrection. This word is only used in the New Testament. More details are given about Paradise and Sheol/Hades by Jesus in Luke 16 than anywhere else in the Bible.

Luke 16:19-31

19 There was a certain rich man, which was clothed in purple and fine linen, and fared sumptuously every day:

20 And there was a certain beggar named Lazarus, which was laid at his gate, full of sores,

21 And desiring to be fed with the crumbs which fell from the rich man's table: moreover the dogs came and licked his sores.

22 And it came to pass, that the beggar died, and was carried by the angels into Abraham's bosom: the rich man also died, and was buried;

23 And in hell (*Sheol*) he lift up his eyes, being in torments, and seeth Abraham afar off, and Lazarus in his bosom.

24 And he cried and said, Father Abraham, have mercy on me, and send Lazarus, that he may dip the tip of his finger in water, and cool my tongue; for I am tormented in this flame.

25 But Abraham said, Son, remember that thou in thy life-time receivedst thy good things, and likewise Lazarus evil things: but now he is comforted, and thou art tormented.

26 And beside all this, between us and you there is a great gulf fixed: so that they which would pass from hence to you cannot; neither can they pass to us, that would come from thence.

27 Then he said, I pray thee therefore, father, that thou wouldest send him to my father's house:

28 For I have five brethren; that he may testify unto them, lest they also come into this place of torment.

29 Abraham saith unto him, They have Moses and the prophets; let them hear them.

30 And he said, Nay, father Abraham: but if one went unto them from the dead, they will repent.

31 And he said unto him, If they hear not Moses and the prophets, neither will they be persuaded, though one rose from the dead.

(KJV)

From these verses, we can see that Sheol/Hades was created with two compartments for departed human souls/spirits.

The torment side, which included fire and flames, was for those who were not "saved." The people were fully conscious of what they had done and the suffering they were currently experiencing. Even though their physical body was in the grave, their soul/spiritual body was still very much in existence and was suffering.

The side of Sheol/Hades called Paradise that provided comfort was also known as Abraham's bosom. This side was for the departed souls/spirit bodies of those who were "saved." They were also fully conscious and were in comfort from the ills of the world.

As stated in verse 26 above, the two compartments were separated by a great gulf that was fixed so that occupants of one side could not go to the other side, though they could be seen and heard.

5) Tartarus – It is believed to be a sub-compartment of the torment side of Sheol/Hades where the angels who sinned (left their first estate) as described in Genesis 6 have been kept since the great flood.

The first estate of an angel, as created, was to be celibate and not to have sexual relations with humans. A portion of the angels who fell with Satan decided to leave that state of celibacy (their first estate) so they could have sexual relations with human women.

Genesis 6:1–8

1 And it came to pass, when men began to multiply on the face of the earth, and daughters were born unto them,

2 That the **sons of God** saw the **daughters of men** that they were fair; and they took them wives of all which they chose.

3 And the Lord said, My spirit shall not always strive with man, for that he also is flesh: yet his days shall be an hundred and twenty years.

4 There were giants in the earth in those days; and also after that, when the sons of God came in unto the daughters of

men, and they bare children to them, the same became mighty men which were of old, men of renown.

5 And God saw that the wickedness of man was great in the earth, and that every imagination of the thoughts of his heart was only evil continually.

6 And it repented the Lord that he had made man on the earth, and it grieved him at his heart.

7 And the Lord said, I will destroy man whom I have created from the face of the earth; both man, and beast, and the creeping thing, and the fowls of the air; for it repenteth me that I have made them.

8 But Noah found grace in the eyes of the Lord.

(KJV)

The "sons of God" in verse 2 are the group of fallen angels who left their first estate and sinned by marrying and having offspring with the "daughters of men" as they selected them. The offspring were hybrids of humans and fallen angels referred to in Hebrew as the *Nephelim*. The English word that is used in verse 4 is "giants."

Jude 6

6 And **the angels which kept not their first estate**, but left their own habitation, he hath reserved in everlasting chains under darkness unto the judgment of the great day.

(KJV)

2 Peter 2:4

4 For if God spared not **the angels that sinned**, but cast them down to **hell** (*Tartarus*), and delivered them into chains of darkness, to be reserved unto judgment;

(KJV)

Although, per Revelation 12, one-third of the created angels rebelled and fell from their original positions, only those who left their first estate and sinned by intermarrying and having offspring with human women are now being kept in everlasting chains under darkness in *Tartarus* until the day of judgment (the Great White Throne Judgment in Revelation 20).

Revelation 12:3–4

3 And there appeared another wonder in heaven; and behold a great red dragon (Satan, originally Lucifer), having seven heads and ten horns, and seven crowns upon his heads.

4 And his tail drew **the third part of the stars of heaven (angels)**, and did cast them to the earth: and the dragon stood before the woman which was ready to be delivered, for to devour her child as soon as it was born.

(KJV)

Revelation 20:11–14

11 And I saw **a great white throne**, and him that sat on it, from whose face the earth and the heaven fled away; and there was found no place for them.

12 And I saw the dead, small and great, stand before God; and the books were opened: and another book was opened, which is the book of life: and the dead were judged out of those things which were written in the books, according to their works.

13 And the sea gave up the dead which were in it; and death and hell delivered up the dead which were in them: and they were judged every man according to their works.

14 And death and hell (*Hades*, **including Tartarus**) were cast into the lake of fire. This is the second death.

(KJV)

6) The Abyss / The Bottomless Pit – This is a part of Sheol/Hades where only three sets of entities/people will temporarily reside – Demonic Beings, The Beast (Antichrist), and Satan and his cohorts.

Demonic Beings

Revelation 9:1–5

1 And the fifth angel sounded, and I saw a star fall from heaven unto the earth: and to him was given the key of the **bottomless pit.**

2 And he opened the bottomless pit; and there arose a smoke out of the pit, as the smoke of a great furnace; and the sun and the air were darkened by reason of the smoke of the pit.

3 **And there came out of the smoke locusts upon the earth: and unto them was given power, as the scorpions of the earth have power.**

4 And it was commanded them that they should not hurt the grass of the earth, neither any green thing, neither any tree; but only those men which have not the seal of God in their foreheads.

5 And to them it was given that they should not kill them, but that they should be tormented five months: and their torment was as the torment of a scorpion, when he striketh a man.

(KJV)

The Beast (Antichrist)

Revelation 17:8

8 The beast that thou sawest was, and is not; and shall ascend out of the bottomless pit, and go into perdition: and they that dwell on the earth shall wonder, whose names were not written in the book of life from the foundation of the world, when they behold the beast that was, and is not, and yet is **(this is the Antichrist)**.

(KJV)

The Antichrist starts the seven-year Tribulation as a natural man who is demonically influenced but is killed after three and a half years. He is bodily resurrected with a soul/spirit that ascends out of the bottomless pit and is immediately indwelt by Satan who had just been cast out of heaven to the earth as the result of the war in heaven between Michael and his angels and Satan (the dragon) and his angels.

Revelation 13:1–5

1 And I stood upon the sand of the sea, and saw a beast rise up out of the sea, having seven heads and ten horns, and upon his horns ten crowns, and upon his heads the name of blasphemy.

2 And the beast which I saw was like unto a leopard, and his feet were as the feet of a bear, and his mouth as the mouth of a lion: and the dragon gave him his power, and his seat, and great authority.

3 And I saw one of his heads as it were wounded to death; and his deadly wound was healed: and all the world wondered after the beast.

4 And they worshipped the dragon which gave power unto the beast: and they worshipped the beast, saying, Who is like unto the beast? who is able to make war with him?

5 And there was given unto him a mouth speaking great things and blasphemies; and power was given unto him to continue forty and two months.

(KJV)

Revelation 13:11–12

11 And I beheld another beast coming up out of the earth; and he had two horns like a lamb, and he spake as a dragon.

12 And he exerciseth all the power of the first beast before him, and causeth the earth and them which dwell therein to worship **the first beast, whose deadly wound was healed.**

(KJV)

Satan and his cohorts

Revelation 20:1–3

1 And I saw an angel come down from heaven, having the key of the bottomless pit and a great chain in his hand.

2 And he laid hold on the dragon, that old serpent, which is the Devil, and Satan, and bound him a thousand years,

3 And cast him into the bottomless pit, and shut him up, and set a seal upon him, that he should deceive the nations no more, till the thousand years should be fulfilled: and after that he must be loosed a little season.

(KJV)

7) Lake of Fire and Brimstone (*Gehenna*) – This will be the final and permanent dwelling place of all the unsaved from the Book of Genesis to the Book of Revelation. Satan, and all the angels who followed him in his rebellion, including the angels who sinned by intermarrying and having offspring with women, will be there as well. The Lake of Fire is also referred to as "outer darkness" in some places.

Matthew 10:28

28 And fear not them which kill the body, but are not able to kill the soul: but rather fear him which is able to destroy both soul and body in **hell** (the Greek word *Gehenna* is used here).

(KJV)

Matthew 25:30

30 And cast ye the unprofitable servant into **outer darkness**: there shall be weeping and gnashing of teeth.

(KJV)

Revelation 20:12–15

12 And I saw the dead, small and great, stand before God; and the books were opened: and another book was opened, which is the book of life: and the dead were judged out of those things which were written in the books, according to their works.

13 And the sea gave up the dead which were in it; and death and hell delivered up the dead which were in them: and they were judged every man according to their works.

14 And death and hell were cast into the **lake of fire**. This is the second death.

15 And whosoever was not found written in the book of life was cast into the **lake of fire.**

(KJV)

Revelation 20:10

10 And the devil that deceived them was cast into the **lake of fire and brimstone**, where the beast and the false prophet are, and shall be tormented day and night for ever and ever.

(KJV)

8) Heaven – The Bible defines three heavens. The first two were created on day 1. From the earth's perspective, Heaven 2 is the universe. Heaven 3 is the abode of God. Heaven 1 was created on day 2 of creation when God divided the waters from the waters and defined that space where the waters were divided as heaven, also called the firmament.

Day 1

Genesis 1:1

1 In the beginning God created the Heaven and the earth.

(KJV)

The word "Heaven" in verse 1 is a <u>plural</u> word in Hebrew; thus, in the New King James Version and other modern translations, it is rendered "Heavens." This would include both Heaven 2 and Heaven 3.

Day 2

Genesis 1:6–8

6 And God said, Let there be a firmament in the midst of the waters, and let it divide the waters from the waters.

7 And God made the firmament, and divided the waters which were under the firmament from the waters which were above the firmament: and it was so.

8 **And God called the firmament Heaven**. And the evening and the morning were the second day.

(KJV)

Heaven in verse 8 is <u>singular</u> and is defined in verse 20, which is the fifth day of creation, as where the birds (fowl) fly.

Genesis 1:20

20 And God said, Let the waters bring forth abundantly the moving creature that hath life, and fowl that may fly above the earth in the open firmament of **heaven**.

(KJV)

It is the Holy Spirit through Paul that confirms to us three heavens.

2 Corinthians 12:1–4

12 It is not expedient for me doubtless to glory. I will come to visions and revelations of the Lord.

2 I knew a man in Christ above fourteen years ago, (whether in the body, I cannot tell; or whether out of the body, I cannot tell: God knoweth) such an one **caught up to the third heaven.**

3 And I knew such a man, (whether in the body, or out of the body, I cannot tell: God knoweth)

4 How that he was caught up into **paradise**, and heard unspeakable words, which it is not lawful for a man to utter.

(KJV)

Paul, in these verses, was referring to himself being stoned to death in Lystra during his first missionary journey. He was brought back to life and after fourteen years finally talks about the experience.

Acts 14:19–20

19 And there came thither certain Jews from Antioch and Iconium, who persuaded the people, and, **having stoned Paul, drew him out of the city, supposing he had been dead.**

20 **Howbeit, as the disciples stood round about him, he rose up,** and came into the city: and the next day he departed with Barnabas to Derbe.

(KJV)

It is the third heaven where God resides. It has been asked that since none of the heavens were here before day 1 of creation, where was God? The good news is that the Bible answers that question.

Isaiah 57:15

15 For thus saith the high and lofty One that inhabiteth **eternity**, whose name is Holy; I dwell in the high and holy place, with him also that is of a contrite and humble spirit, to revive the spirit of the humble, and to revive the heart of the contrite ones.

(KJV)

God alone inhabited "**eternity**" before anything, visible and invisible, was created. This includes all three heavens.

With all the locations defined, we will now focus our attention on their occupants over time, with the understanding that time was also created in verse 1 of Genesis. In fact, God created Space, Matter, and Time simultaneously. Neither would be able to exist on its own. Space with nothing in it would be meaningless. Matter without somewhere to put it would be equally meaningless. Time without the means of measuring or sensing its progression through changes in space or matter would be just as meaningless.

Nevertheless, let's move forward.

Chapter 4

In the Beginning

In the beginning, God created everything good and even summed it all up as very good.

Genesis 1:31

31 And God saw every thing that he had made, and, behold, it was **very good**. And the evening and the morning were the sixth day.

(KJV)

Everything visible and invisible, physical, and spiritual was very good. Lucifer was the anointed cherub that covereth (Ezekiel 28:14), and all the angels were in alignment with God. All the animal kingdom, birds, and sea life were in harmony. Man was in complete harmony with God and all that God had placed under his dominion. No wars, no famine, no pestilences, no sickness, no diseases, and no death.

Although *Sheol, Hades,* Paradise, *Tartarus,* the Lake of Fire, and the grave were all in place, they were all empty. The third heaven was populated with God and the angels, who at times would visit the earth. In fact, God came down and communed with Adam on earth as well.

Genesis 3:8

8 And they heard the voice of **the Lord God walking in the garden in the cool of the day**: and Adam and his wife hid themselves from the presence of the Lord God amongst the trees of the garden.

(KJV)

Sometime between Genesis 2 and Genesis 3, Lucifer (Son of the Morning) fell from **the position** of being the anointed cherub that covereth to that of Satan (Adversary). This is so significant that it is recorded twice in the Bible.

Isaiah 14:12–17

12 How art thou fallen from heaven, O Lucifer, son of the morning! how art thou cut down to the ground, which didst weaken the nations!

13 For thou hast said in thine heart, I will ascend into heaven, I will exalt my throne above the stars of God: I will sit also upon the mount of the congregation, in the sides of the north:

14 I will ascend above the heights of the clouds; I will be like the most High.

15 Yet thou shalt be brought down to hell, to the sides of the pit.

16 They that see thee shall narrowly look upon thee, and consider thee, saying, Is this the man that made the earth to tremble, that did shake kingdoms;

17 That made the world as a wilderness, and destroyed the cities thereof; that opened not the house of his prisoners?

(KJV)

Ezekiel 28:11–19

11 Moreover the word of the Lord came unto me, saying,

12 Son of man, take up a lamentation upon the king of Tyrus, and say unto him, Thus saith the Lord God; Thou sealest up the sum, full of wisdom, and perfect in beauty.

13 Thou hast been in Eden the garden of God; every precious stone was thy covering, the sardius, topaz, and the diamond, the beryl, the onyx, and the jasper, the sapphire, the emerald, and the carbuncle, and gold: the workmanship of thy tabrets and of thy pipes was prepared in thee in the day that thou wast created.

14 Thou art the anointed cherub that covereth; and I have set thee so: thou wast upon the holy mountain of God; thou hast walked up and down in the midst of the stones of fire.

15 Thou wast perfect in thy ways from the day that thou wast created, till iniquity was found in thee.

16 By the multitude of thy merchandise they have filled the midst of thee with violence, and thou hast sinned: therefore I will cast thee as profane out of the mountain of God: and I will destroy thee, O covering cherub, from the midst of the stones of fire.

17 Thine heart was lifted up because of thy beauty, thou hast corrupted thy wisdom by reason of thy brightness: I

will cast thee to the ground, I will lay thee before kings, that they may behold thee.

18 Thou hast defiled thy sanctuaries by the multitude of thine iniquities, by the iniquity of thy traffick; therefore will I bring forth a fire from the midst of thee, it shall devour thee, and I will bring thee to ashes upon the earth in the sight of all them that behold thee.

19 All they that know thee among the people shall be astonished at thee: thou shalt be a terror, and never shalt thou be any more.

(KJV)

At the rebellion and fall of Lucifer, one-third of the angels aligned themselves with Satan but still had and have access to heaven.

Revelation 12:3–4

3 And there appeared another wonder in heaven; and behold a great red dragon, having seven heads and ten horns, and seven crowns upon his heads.

4 **And his tail drew the third part of the stars of heaven,** and did cast them to the earth: and the dragon stood before the woman which was ready to be delivered, for to devour her child as soon as it was born.

(KJV)

Job 1:6–7

6 Now there was a day when the **sons of God** came to present themselves before the Lord, and **Satan** came also among them.

7 And the Lord said unto Satan, Whence comest thou? Then Satan answered the Lord, and said, From going to and fro in the earth, and from walking up and down in it.

(KJV)

Revelation 12:7–13

7 And there was **war in heaven**: Michael and his angels fought against the dragon; and the dragon fought and his angels,

8 And prevailed not; neither was their place found any more in heaven.

9 **And the great dragon** was cast out, that old serpent, called the Devil, and Satan, which deceiveth the whole world: he **was cast out into the earth, and his angels were cast out with him.**

10 And I heard a loud voice saying in heaven, Now is come salvation, and strength, and the kingdom of our God, and the power of his Christ: **for the accuser of our brethren is cast down, which accused them before our God day and night.**

11 And they overcame him by the blood of the Lamb, and by the word of their testimony; and they loved not their lives unto the death.

12 **Therefore rejoice, ye heavens, and ye that dwell in them. Woe to the inhabiters of the earth and of the sea! for the devil is come down unto you, having great wrath, because he knoweth that he hath but a short time.**

13 And when the dragon saw that he was cast unto the earth, he persecuted the woman which brought forth the man child.

(KJV)

In Job 1:6 above, the sons of God are angels, and when they presented themselves before the Lord, Satan was among them, even though he and God were now adversaries.

In Revelation 12:7–13, a war breaks out in the third heaven where the dragon (Satan) and his angels fight against Michael and his angels. Satan and his angels lose the war and will be for the first time permanently cast out of all the heavens (3, 2, and 1) and will be limited to planet earth only. Verse 10 tells us that Satan was before the throne of God (in heaven) day and night, accusing us when we do wrong, before the war takes place. Verse 12 tells us that when Satan realizes he has been permanently cast out of heaven, he will become exceedingly angry (great wrath) because he knows he has but a short time to vent his wrath (three and a half years – during the Great Tribulation) and decides to take out his anger on the woman (Israel). This whole scenario would make no sense if Satan was cast out of heaven long, long ago. These verses also tell us that Satan and his angels will have access to all three heavens until the beginning of the Great Tribulation (the last three and a half years of the seven-year Tribulation Period).

Though the angels, including fallen angels, had access to the earth, heavens 1 and 2, and the third heaven, none of the angels were bound in Tartarus or the Lake of Fire and Brimstone at this time. They were free to roam.

Since God knows all things, from the beginning to the end, even before the creation, He already knew about the fall of Lucifer and the third of the angels, the fall of man, the intermarriage of some of the fallen angels with women, and death before any of these actually happened. Thus, included in the six days of creation were places, both temporary and permanent, for them all.

Isaiah 46:9–10

9 Remember the former things of old: for I am God, and there is none else; I am God, and there is none like me,

10 **Declaring the end from the beginning**, and from ancient times the things that are not yet done, saying, My counsel shall stand, and I will do all my pleasure:

(KJV)

Matthew 25:41

41 Then shall he say also unto them on the left hand, Depart from me, ye cursed, into everlasting fire, **prepared for the devil and his angels**:

(KJV)

When God ceased creating on day 7 of the creation week, all places, though some were empty (waiting to be occupied), were created as well. This is truly intelligent design demonstrated by the Everlasting, All-Knowing, Everywhere-Present, All-Powerful God. May He be worshipped and praised forever and ever.

Now let's start on the road to see how all this plays out.

Chapter 5

The First Deaths

Up to the point when the first death took place, Sheol/Hades/ Paradise, the grave, Tartarus, and the Lake of Fire were all empty. This, however, was about to change.

Adam and Eve were living peaceably in the garden of Eden until the Serpent, indwelt by Satan, deceived Eve and she ate of the fruit God had forbidden them to eat. God told Adam that the day he would eat of the forbidden fruit, he would surely die. For Adam and Eve, this referred to spiritual death. Death in its simplest definition means "separation." So the day Adam would eat of the forbidden fruit, both he and Eve would be spiritually separated from God. Scripture tells us that Adam lived 930 years before he physically died (Genesis 5:5). Physical death is when the soul/spirit separates from the body. So, though Adam and Eve spiritually died the moment they ate the forbidden fruit, Adam did not physically die until he was 930 years old. The Bible does not tell us how long Eve physically lived.

Genesis 2:15–17

15 And the Lord God took the man, and put him into the garden of Eden to dress it and to keep it.

16 And the Lord God commanded the man, saying, Of every tree of the garden thou mayest freely eat:

17 But of the tree of the knowledge of good and evil, thou shalt not eat of it: for in the day that thou eatest thereof thou shalt surely die.

(KJV)

Genesis 3:1–6

1 Now the serpent was more subtil than any beast of the field which the Lord God had made. And he said unto the woman, Yea, hath God said, Ye shall not eat of every tree of the garden?

2 And the woman said unto the serpent, We may eat of the fruit of the trees of the garden:

3 But of the fruit of the tree which is in the midst of the garden, God hath said, Ye shall not eat of it, neither shall ye touch it, lest ye die.

4 And the serpent said unto the woman, Ye shall not surely die:

5 For God doth know that in the day ye eat thereof, then your eyes shall be opened, and ye shall be as gods, knowing good and evil.

6 And when the woman saw that the tree was good for food, and that it was pleasant to the eyes, and a tree to be desired to make one wise, she took of the fruit thereof, and did eat, and gave also unto her husband with her; and he did eat.

(KJV)

After Adam and Eve had become sinners, being spiritually separated from God, by the eating of the forbidden fruit, God made a temporary atonement (covering) for their sin by killing some animals and using their skins to cover their naked bodies. This event is significant since it notes the first physical deaths in the Bible.

The Bible does not indicate that animals have **eternal** souls or are spiritual beings. They do, however, possess bodies and souls while the body lives. So when God made for Adam and Eve coats of skin, the animals physically died, and their bodies (with the omission of the coats of skin) went to the grave. **Thus, the first occupants of the grave were animals that returned to the dust from which they were made.**

Genesis 3:20–21

20 And Adam called his wife's name Eve; because she was the mother of all living.

21 Unto Adam also and to his wife did the Lord God make **coats of skins**, and clothed them.

(KJV)

As you can see, in summary, the first deaths were animals for the temporary atonement of the sins of Adam and Eve, in addition to providing clothing for their naked bodies.

The Grave is no longer empty.

Let's go a little further in the Book of Genesis, which records the first human death.

Although Adam and Eve died spiritually when they ate of the forbidden fruit, they had not died physically. And though animals were killed in the garden of Eden to temporarily atone for the sins of

Adam and Eve, since they have no eternal soul/spirit, their bodies simply went to the grave. **All the other places (Sheol/Hades/ Paradise, Tartarus, and the Lake of Fire) were still empty.**

This changes with the first death (by murder) of a human, namely, Abel.

Genesis 4:1–11

1 And Adam knew Eve his wife; and she conceived, and bare Cain, and said, I have gotten a man from the Lord.

2 And she again bare his brother Abel. And Abel was a keeper of sheep, but Cain was a tiller of the ground.

3 And in process of time it came to pass, that Cain brought of the fruit of the ground an offering unto the Lord.

4 And Abel, he also brought of the firstlings of his flock and of the fat thereof. And the Lord had respect unto Abel and to his offering:

5 But unto Cain and to his offering he had not respect. And Cain was very wroth, and his countenance fell.

6 And the Lord said unto Cain, Why art thou wroth? and why is thy countenance fallen?

7 If thou doest well, shalt thou not be accepted? and if thou doest not well, sin lieth at the door. And unto thee shall be his desire, and thou shalt rule over him.

8 And Cain talked with Abel his brother: and it came to pass, when they were in the field, that **Cain rose up against Abel his brother, and slew him.**

9 And the Lord said unto Cain, Where is Abel thy brother? And he said, I know not: Am I my brother's keeper?

10 And he said, What hast thou done? the voice of thy brother's blood crieth unto me from the ground.

11 And now art thou cursed from the earth, which hath opened her mouth to receive thy brother's blood from thy hand;

(KJV)

As a result of Abel's physical death, **the population of the Grave increased by one**, but since Abel has an eternal soul/spirit, they are deposited in *Sheol/Hades*, namely, Paradise, the non-torment side. That is because this event occurred before the resurrection of Jesus, which was thousands of years away.

In any case, Abel was the first man who populated *Sheol/Hades*, on the Paradise side, where he resided alone for a while.

It is sobering to know that God had already prepared a place (during the creation week) for Abel's soul/spirit to go before he died. Our God is awesome!

Chapter 6

The First Man in Heaven

In Genesis Chapter 5, we are given a genealogy of Adam from the beginning to the great flood. In that genealogy, we are introduced to a man named Enoch. Enoch was the seventh generation of Adam and had a very close relationship with God.

Genesis 5:18–24

18 And Jared lived an hundred sixty and two years, and he begat Enoch:

19 And Jared lived after he begat Enoch eight hundred years, and begat sons and daughters:

20 And all the days of Jared were nine hundred sixty and two years: and he died.

21 And Enoch lived sixty and five years, and begat Methuselah:

22 And Enoch walked with God after he begat Methuselah three hundred years, and begat sons and daughters:

23 And all the days of Enoch were three hundred sixty and five years:

24 And Enoch walked with God: and he was not; for God took him.

(KJV)

When Enoch was sixty-five years old, after the birth of Methuselah whose name means "when he dies, it will come," he began walking with God. Since Enoch named his son Methuselah, it could be that God revealed something to him that drew him very close to God. In any regard, Enoch walked with God until he was 365 years old.

What is interesting is that the Bible did not say that Enoch died but rather God "took" him. Another word for "took" is "translated." God translated him from life on earth to life in heaven. Hebrews 11 says it as follows:

Hebrews 11:5

5 By faith Enoch was translated that he should not see death; and was not found, because God had translated him: for before his translation he had this testimony, that he pleased God.

(KJV)

Enoch pleased God so much that God revealed futuristic events to him, maybe even the flood that was to come.

Jude 14–15

14 And Enoch also, the seventh from Adam, prophesied of these, saying, Behold, the Lord cometh with ten thousands of his saints,

15 To execute judgment upon all, and to convince all that are ungodly among them of all their ungodly deeds which they have ungodly committed, and of all their hard speeches which ungodly sinners have spoken against him.

(KJV)

As a result of Enoch's translation, he became the first Man to inhabit heaven. I know some say a man cannot go to heaven in his natural, physical body and Jesus said no man had ascended into heaven and had seen God.

May I suggest that since God, who is unlimited in power, decided to translate Enoch, surely He could have changed Enoch's body to live in heaven. Additionally, Jesus said in John 14, "In my Father's House are many mansions (rooms) besides the Throne Room." It could be where Enoch still may be residing, in one of the rooms in heaven, having never seen God in His pure form. Moreover, Enoch did not ascend to heaven on his own; it was God who came and took him.

Only God knows what and how He did what He did, but God certainly translated Enoch to be with Him.

John 3:13

13 And no man hath ascended up to heaven, but he that came down from heaven, even the Son of man which is in heaven.

(KJV)

John 1:18

18 No man hath seen God at any time; the only begotten Son, which is in the bosom of the Father, he hath declared him.

(KJV)

1 Corinthians 15:50

50 Now this I say, brethren, that flesh and blood cannot inherit the kingdom of God; neither doth corruption inherit incorruption.

(KJV)

Yet Hebrews 11:5 says God translated Enoch to heaven. Enoch did not ascend to heaven on his own, but rather God came and translated him.

So at this point, we have the Grave, Sheol, and Heaven being occupied by Man (Abel – Grave/Paradise; Enoch – Heaven). All other areas are still empty but are reserved for habitation.

Chapter 7

The Occupying of Tartarus

The killing of animals provided a temporary atonement for the sins of Adam and Eve (providing them clothing), thus first populating the Grave (Gen 3:21), and the murder of Abel by Cain (Gen 4:8) further populated the Grave and also Sheol (Paradise). Therefore, death was introduced into both the animal world and Man.

The second murder of a human is recorded in Genesis 4:23 by Lamech.

Genesis 4:23

> 23 And Lamech said unto his wives, Adah and Zillah, Hear my voice; ye wives of Lamech, hearken unto my speech: for I have **slain a man** to my wounding, and a young man to my hurt.

> (KJV)

Lamech said he killed a young man for both hitting and wounding him. This will place another body in the Grave and the second person in Sheol. Since we can't be dogmatic here on the spiritual perspective of the young man, we cannot determine which side of Sheol his soul/spirit went to. Since the occupants of Sheol can see and hear each other per Luke 16:22–31, Abel is aware that he no longer occupies Sheol alone.

This will be the template for every human who dies before the resurrection of Jesus. Their bodies will be placed in the Grave, but their soul/spirit would go to Sheol. Their spiritual perspective will determine which side of Sheol they would go.

Up to Genesis 6, the reproduction of humans was always between a man and a woman. Since God made the decree that every species is to reproduce after their own kind, the resultant of the union of a man and a woman would be 100 percent human.

Genesis 1:20–28

20 And God said, Let the waters bring forth abundantly the moving creature that hath life, and fowl that may fly above the earth in the open firmament of heaven.

21 And God created great whales, and every living creature that moveth, which the waters brought forth abundantly, **after their kind**, and every winged fowl **after his kind**: and God saw that it was good.

22 And God blessed them, saying, Be fruitful, and multiply, and fill the waters in the seas, and let fowl multiply in the earth.

23 And the evening and the morning were the fifth day.

24 And God said, Let the earth bring forth the living creature **after his kind**, cattle, and creeping thing, and beast of the earth **after his kind**: and it was so.

25 And God made the beast of the earth **after his kind**, and cattle **after their kind**, and every thing that creepeth

upon the earth **after his kind**: and God saw that it was good.

26 And God said, Let us make man in our image, after our likeness: and let them have dominion over the fish of the sea, and over the fowl of the air, and over the cattle, and over all the earth, and over every creeping thing that creepeth upon the earth.

27 So God created man in his own image, in the image of God created he him; male and female created he them.

28 And God blessed them, and God said unto them**, Be fruit-ful, and multiply**, and replenish the earth, and subdue it: and have dominion over the fish of the sea, and over the fowl of the air, and over every living thing that moveth upon the earth.

(KJV)

However, in Genesis 6, we see a deviation in the human reproductive process. We see the "sons of God" choosing wives and having off-spring by the "daughters of men." The "sons of God" are fallen angels per Revelation 12 and Job 1.

Revelation 12:3–4

3 And there appeared another wonder in heaven; and behold a great red dragon, having seven heads and ten horns, and seven crowns upon his heads.

4 And his tail drew the **third part of the stars of heaven**, and did cast them to the earth: and the dragon stood before the woman which was ready to be delivered, for to devour her child as soon as it was born.

(KJV)

Job 1:6–7

6 Now there was a day when the **sons of God** came to present themselves before the Lord, and Satan came also among them.

7 And the Lord said unto Satan, Whence comest thou? Then Satan answered the Lord, and said, From going to and fro in the earth, and from walking up and down in it.

(KJV)

The offspring of a sexual union between an unsaved man or woman would still be human since they are both of the human "kind." The offspring of the "sons of God" with the "daughters of men," however, were not completely human or angel and are called in Hebrew *Nephilim*, which means "fallen ones or earth born."

Angels were not to cross the human boundary by having intercourse with them. Though one-third of the created angels sided with Satan in the rebellion, they were to respect the angel/human boundary. The angels, as created in their first estate, could not and do not reproduce.

Unfortunately, some of the fallen angels did willfully **leave their first estate** to marry and have children by human women, thus sinning.

Jude 6

6 And the angels which **kept not their first estate**, but left their own habitation, he hath reserved in everlasting chains under darkness unto the judgment of the great day.

(KJV)

2 Peter 2:4–5

4 For if God spared not the **angels that sinned**, but cast them down to hell (Tartarus), and delivered them into chains of darkness, to be reserved unto judgment;

5 And spared not the old world, but saved Noah the eighth person, a preacher of righteousness, bringing in the flood upon the world of the ungodly;

(KJV)

Genesis 6:1–4

1 And it came to pass, when men began to multiply on the face of the earth, and daughters were born unto them,

2 That the sons of God saw the daughters of men that they were fair; and they took them wives of all which they chose.

3 And the Lord said, My spirit shall not always strive with man, for that he also is flesh: yet his days shall be an hundred and twenty years.

4 There were **giants (*Nephilim*) in the earth in those days; and also after that**, when the sons of God came in unto the daughters of men, and they bare children to them, the same became mighty men which were of old, men of renown.

(KJV)

The scriptures above also show the process and timing when this event occurred. Jude 6 says **some** of the fallen angels left their first estate, thus allowing them to have physical intercourse with women.

2 Peter 4–5 indicates the sinning of the angels occurred before the flood, and Genesis 6:1–4 tells us what the sin was.

I will deal with the *Nephilim* a little later, but now I want to focus on the fallen angels who sinned. It is quite clear from 2 Peter 2:4 that God cast them into **hell (Tartarus)** to be kept there until the day of judgment (the Great White Throne Judgment; see Revelation 20:11–15).

In God's wisdom, He chose not to place the sinning angels in the same area of Sheol/Hades with the souls/spirits of Man but rather in a special lower compartment of Sheol (called **Tartarus** in Greek) in chains of darkness. In Sheol, as described in Luke 16, there is light, and the occupants can see each other there. However, in Tartarus, the sinning angels are in complete darkness.

Thus, the sinning angels were the first and only occupants of Tartarus. They are in complete isolation and darkness, only to be released for the Great White Throne Judgment and then to be cast into the Lake of Fire (*Gehenna*), which is also described as outer darkness. See 2 Peter 4–5 above and the scriptures below.

Matthew 25:30

30 And cast ye the unprofitable servant into **outer darkness**: there shall be weeping and gnashing of teeth.

(KJV)

Matthew 5:29

29 And if thy right eye offend thee, pluck it out, and cast it from thee: for it is profitable for thee that one of thy mem-

bers should perish, and not that thy whole body should be cast into **hell (*Gehenna*).**

(KJV)

Praise God that He has given us a choice to spend eternity with Him or spend eternity in Gehenna. The choice is yours.

Chapter 8

The Great Flood

After the "sons of God" (fallen angels who left their first estate) came down marrying and having children with the "daughters of men" (women), the inhabitants of earth became extremely violent, and evil was constant and everywhere.

Genesis 6:1–8

1 And it came to pass, when men began to multiply on the face of the earth, and daughters were born unto them,

2 That the sons of God saw the daughters of men that they were fair; and they took them wives of all which they chose.

3 And the Lord said, My spirit shall not always strive with man, for that he also is flesh: yet his days shall be an hundred and twenty years.

4 There were giants in the earth in those days; and also after that, when the sons of God came in unto the daughters of men, and they bare children to them, the same became mighty men which were of old, men of renown.

5 And God saw that the **wickedness of man** was great in the earth, **and that every imagination of the thoughts of his heart was only evil continually.**

6 And it repented the Lord that he had made man on the earth, and it grieved him at his heart.

7 And the Lord said, I will destroy man whom I have created from the face of the earth; both man, and beast, and the creeping thing, and the fowls of the air; for it repenteth me that I have made them.

8 But Noah found grace in the eyes of the Lord.

(KJV)

Because of the evilness and violence, God decided to destroy both Man and the rest of the things He created on planet earth. However, as we will see, God will save a remnant—eight humans, two of each kind of unclean animals, and seven of each kind of clean animals. God would save them from the worldwide flood through an Ark that Noah was instructed to build.

The Ark was not to be a motor-driven vehicle but simply a haven for the remnant through the judgment of God by the universal flood. The Ark reminds us of a picture of Christ. All who are in Christ (a remnant of total humanity) are in a haven from God's judgment on earth by fire the next time.

2 Peter 3:3–13

3 Knowing this first, that there shall come in the last days scoffers, walking after their own lusts,

4 And saying, Where is the promise of his coming? for since the fathers fell asleep, all things continue as they were from the beginning of the creation.

5 For this they willingly are ignorant of, that by the word of God the heavens were of old, and the earth standing out of the water and in the water:

6 Whereby the world that then was, being overflowed with water, perished:

7 But the heavens and the earth, which are now, by the same word are kept in store, reserved unto fire against the day of judgment and perdition of ungodly men.

8 But, beloved, be not ignorant of this one thing, that one day is with the Lord as a thousand years, and a thousand years as one day.

9 The Lord is not slack concerning his promise, as some men count slackness; but is longsuffering to us-ward, not willing that any should perish, but that all should come to repentance.

10 But the day of the Lord will come as a thief in the night; in the which the heavens shall pass away with a great noise, and the elements shall melt with fervent heat, the earth also and the works that are therein shall be burned up.

11 Seeing then that all these things shall be dissolved, what manner of persons ought ye to be in all holy conversation and godliness,

12 Looking for and hasting unto the coming of the day of God, wherein the heavens being on fire shall be dissolved, and the elements shall melt with fervent heat?

13 Nevertheless we, according to his promise, look for new heavens and a new earth, wherein dwelleth righteousness.

(KJV)

One hundred twenty years after God's announcement to destroy the earth in which the Ark was built, God unleashed floodwaters by rain from above for forty days and forty nights in conjunction with the fountains of the deep being broken up. As a result, everything alive that did not live in the waters was killed. This included Man, the hybrid of Man/Angel (Nephilim), beasts, fowls, and creeping things.

The angels who had sinned were cast and bound in Tartarus as stated earlier. The bodies of all of mankind, including the bodies of the Nephilim, were buried in the Grave, along with the bodies of the land animals, fowl, and creeping things.

The souls/spirits of men and women who died in the flood were placed in Sheol; however, the souls/spirits of the Nephilim presented a different issue. Since the Nephilim were a mixture (hybrid) of man and fallen angel, they were not placed in Tartarus (the abode of the angels who sinned) or Sheol (the abode of humans who had died).

So where did the souls/spirits of the Nephilim go? Some believe they were left to roam the earth as what we refer to as demons. Demons are evil spirits that seek bodies to inhabit since they were conceived in bodies that had been destroyed in the great flood. Angels do not seek such.

Matthew 8:28–32

28 And when he was come to the other side into the country of the Gergesenes, there met him two possessed with devils, coming out of the tombs, exceeding fierce, so that no man might pass by that way.

29 And, behold, they cried out, saying, What have we to do with thee, Jesus, thou Son of God? art thou come hither to torment us before the time?

30 And there was a good way off from them an herd of many swine feeding.

31 So the devils besought him, saying, If thou cast us out, suffer us to go away into the herd of swine.

32 And he said unto them, Go. And when they were come out, they went into the herd of swine: and, behold, the whole herd of swine ran violently down a steep place into the sea, and perished in the waters.

(KJV)

Matthew 12:43–45

43 When the unclean spirit is gone out of a man, he walketh through dry places, seeking rest, and findeth none.

44 Then he saith, I will return into my house from whence I came out; and when he is come, he findeth it empty, swept, and garnished.

45 Then goeth he, and taketh with himself seven other spirits more wicked than himself, and they enter in and dwell there: and the last state of that man is worse than the first. Even so shall it be also unto this wicked generation.

(KJV)

Before concluding this chapter, I need to bring up another possibility that is rarely discussed. Most believe the fallen sons of God who married and had children by human women started to do so when Noah was given the word that 120 years had been determined (Genesis 6:1–3). However, the biblical text does not tell us when they actually started this process. By reading the words of Genesis 6:9 where Noah is described as being "perfect" in his generation, it is believed that Noah was not contaminated by the genes of the Nephilim. This would infer the sons of God came down to the daughters of men in plenty of time that Noah and his generation could have been contaminated.

Some believe they started that process back in the days of Enoch or even before then. That would give Noah's generation plenty of time for the possibility of being contaminated by the fallen angel's genes or even the genes of the children who were the offspring of the Nephilim.

Hardly do we consider that the Nephilim may have had children. If they did, they would also be hybrids (part angel and part human). They, along with the Nephilim, would also suffer a similar fate in the great flood. Their bodies would be deposited in the grave, but maybe their souls/spirits went into the bottomless pit, where they are to be released in the Great Tribulation at the blowing of the fifth trumpet (Revelation 9:1–11). These are truly demonic spirits being released, but there is no mention in the Book of Revelation as to how they got there in the first place.

Since the Nephilim and their offspring would both yield demonic spirits from their bodily deaths, it could be that the souls/spirits of the Nephilim are presently in the bottomless pit but the souls/spirits of their offspring are free to roam as evil spirits and demonic spirits today. God knows.

Genesis 6:1–3

1 And it came to pass, when men began to multiply on the face of the earth, and daughters were born unto them,

2 That the sons of God saw the daughters of men that they were fair; and they took them wives of all which they chose.

3 And the Lord said, My spirit shall not always strive with man, for that he also is flesh: yet his days shall be **an hundred and twenty years.**

(KJV)

Genesis 6:9

9 These are the generations of Noah: Noah was a just man and perfect in his generations, and Noah walked with God.

(KJV)

Revelation 9:1–11

1 And the fifth angel sounded, and I saw a star fall from heaven unto the earth: and to him was given the key of the bottomless pit.

2 And he opened the bottomless pit; and there arose a smoke out of the pit, as the smoke of a great furnace; and the sun and the air were darkened by reason of the smoke of the pit.

3 And there came out of the smoke locusts upon the earth: and unto them was given power, as the scorpions of the earth have power.

4 And it was commanded them that they should not hurt the grass of the earth, neither any green thing, neither any tree; but only those men which have not the seal of God in their foreheads.

5 And to them it was given that they should not kill them, but that they should be tormented five months: and their torment was as the torment of a scorpion, when he striketh a man.

6 And in those days shall men seek death, and shall not find it; and shall desire to die, and death shall flee from them.

7 And the shapes of the locusts were like unto horses prepared unto battle; and on their heads were as it were crowns like gold, and their faces were as the faces of men.

8 And they had hair as the hair of women, and their teeth were as the teeth of lions.

9 And they had breastplates, as it were breastplates of iron; and the sound of their wings was as the sound of chariots of many horses running to battle.

10 And they had tails like unto scorpions, and there were stings in their tails: and their power was to hurt men five months.

11 And they had a king over them, which is the angel of the bottomless pit, whose name in the Hebrew tongue is Abaddon, but in the Greek tongue hath his name Apollyon.

(KJV)

So after the great flood, a great number of bodies were now in the Grave. A great company of human souls/spirits became additional occupants of Sheol/Hades, and the souls/spirits of the Nephilim and their offspring were left roaming the earth, seeking refuge and rest in bodies, whether they be man (preferably) or beast and one or the other being confined in the bottomless pit. The ones left to roam had to do so for a while until all were released from the Ark of Safety and began to multiply on the face of the earth again.

We should all thank God that He preserved a remnant to repopulate the earth. Through the remnant, over time, the seed of the woman, the Redeemer, the Messiah, Jesus of Nazareth, would be born to take away the sin of the world that whosoever would believe in Him would have everlasting life with God.

John 1:29–34

29 The next day John seeth Jesus coming unto him, and saith, Behold the Lamb of God, which taketh away the sin of the world.

30 This is he of whom I said, After me cometh a man which is preferred before me: for he was before me.

31 And I knew him not: but that he should be made manifest to Israel, therefore am I come baptizing with water.

32 And John bare record, saying, I saw the Spirit descending from heaven like a dove, and it abode upon him.

33 And I knew him not: but he that sent me to baptize with water, the same said unto me, Upon whom thou shalt see the Spirit descending, and remaining on him, the same is he which baptizeth with the Holy Ghost.

34 And I saw, and bare record that this is the Son of God.

(KJV)

John 3:16

16 For God so loved the world, that he gave his only begotten Son, that whosoever believeth in him should not perish, but have everlasting life.

(KJV)

We should also reiterate that through the repopulation of the earth by the remnant, demonic spirits from the Nephilim or their offspring had new bodies to occupy. Not all humans, but some, for thousands of demonic spirits can occupy the same body.

Mark 5:6–9

6 But when he saw Jesus afar off, he ran and worshipped him,

7 And cried with a loud voice, and said, What have I to do with thee, Jesus, thou Son of the most high God? I adjure thee by God, that thou torment me not.

8 For he said unto him, Come out of the man, thou unclean spirit.

9 And he asked him, What is thy name? And he answered, saying, **My name is Legion**: for we are many.

(KJV)

Legion represented six thousand. It may be hard to see how six thousand demonic spirits can occupy one person, but there is a lot we don't understand about the spiritual realm.

Thank God that at the Great White Throne Judgment, demonic spirits will finally be placed in their permanent dwelling place—the Lake of Fire (Gehenna).

Chapter 9

The Exceptions

After the Great Flood, the cycle of human life and death would continue in this fashion. A person would be born, live their life, and eventually die. At death, their bodies would be placed in the Grave, and the souls/spirits would go to Sheol/Hades, either on the torment side or the comfort side, later to be known as Abraham's bosom. The side of Sheol/Hades they would go to would be determined by their relationship with the Almighty God.

Two exceptions to this cycle are worth mentioning. The first is Moses and the second is Elijah.

Moses was born, lived his life, died, and was buried by God. His soul/spirit went to the comfort side of Sheol/Hades (Paradise) for a short period but was resurrected.

Deuteronomy 34:1–7

34 And Moses went up from the plains of Moab unto the mountain of Nebo, to the top of Pisgah, that is over against Jericho. And the Lord shewed him all the land of Gilead, unto Dan,

2 And all Naphtali, and the land of Ephraim, and Manasseh, and all the land of Judah, unto the utmost sea,

3 And the south, and the plain of the valley of Jericho, the city of palm trees, unto Zoar.

4 And the Lord said unto him, This is the land which I sware unto Abraham, unto Isaac, and unto Jacob, saying, I will give it unto thy seed: I have caused thee to see it with thine eyes, but thou shalt not go over thither.

5 So Moses the servant of the Lord died there in the land of Moab, according to the word of the Lord.

6 And he buried him in a valley in the land of Moab, over against Beth-peor: but no man knoweth of his sepulchre unto this day.

7 And Moses was an hundred and twenty years old when he died: his eye was not dim, nor his natural force abated.

(KJV)

The scripture above records the death and burial of Moses. However, Moses is resurrected, and there is a dispute between the Archangel Michael and Satan over his body. As noted in verse 6 above, no person knew where Moses's body was, but Michael and Satan knew.

Jude 9

9 Yet Michael the archangel, when contending with the devil he disputed about the **body of Moses**, durst not bring against him a railing accusation, but said, The Lord rebuke thee.

(KJV)

This is confirmed at the transfiguration of Jesus, where two individuals appeared, Moses and Elijah. Both men were alive and well, talking with Jesus.

Matthew 17:1–5

1 And after six days Jesus taketh Peter, James, and John his brother, and bringeth them up into an high mountain apart,

2 And was transfigured before them: and his face did shine as the sun, and his raiment was white as the light.

3 **And, behold, there appeared unto them Moses and Elias talking with him.**

4 Then answered Peter, and said unto Jesus, Lord, it is good for us to be here: if thou wilt, let us make here three tabernacles; one for thee, and one for Moses, and one for Elias.

5 While he yet spake, behold, a bright cloud overshadowed them: and behold a voice out of the cloud, which said, This is my beloved Son, in whom I am well pleased; hear ye him.

(KJV)

It is believed by several biblical scholars that the two witnesses in Revelation 11 who prophesied in Jerusalem during the first half of the tribulation are also Moses and Elijah based on their ministries when they were initially on earth.

Revelation 11:3–13

3 And I will give power unto **my two witnesses**, and they shall prophesy a thousand two hundred and threescore days, clothed in sackcloth.

4 These are the two olive trees, and the two candlesticks standing before the God of the earth.

5 And if any man will hurt them, fire proceedeth out of their mouth, and devoureth their enemies: and if any man will hurt them, he must in this manner be killed.

6 These have power to shut heaven, that it rain not in the days of their prophecy: and have power over waters to turn them to blood, and to smite the earth with all plagues, as often as they will.

7 And when they shall have finished their testimony, **the beast that ascendeth out of the bottomless pit shall make war against them, and shall overcome them, and kill them.**

8 And their dead bodies shall lie in the street of the great city, which spiritually is called Sodom and Egypt, where also our Lord was crucified.

9 And they of the people and kindreds and tongues and nations shall see their dead bodies three days and an half, and shall not suffer their dead bodies to be put in graves.

10 And they that dwell upon the earth shall rejoice over them, and make merry, and shall send gifts one to another; because these two prophets tormented them that dwelt on the earth.

11 And after three days and an half the Spirit of life from God entered into them, and they stood upon their feet; and great fear fell upon them which saw them.

12 And they heard a great voice from heaven saying unto them, Come up hither. And they ascended up to heaven in a cloud; and their enemies beheld them.

13 And the same hour was there a great earthquake, and the tenth part of the city fell, and in the earthquake were slain of men seven thousand: and the remnant were affrighted, and gave glory to the God of heaven.

(KJV)

Notice in verse 9 the reference to their dead "bodies" not being put in graves. So where is Moses today? The answer to that question is found in Zechariah 4 and is referenced in Revelation 11. He is in heaven today with God. He, along with Elijah, came back briefly to talk with Jesus on the Mount of Transfiguration, but they were taken back. They will both come back to earth to fulfill their ministries during the first half of the tribulation.

Zechariah 4:11–14

11 Then answered I, and said unto him, What are these two olive trees upon the right side of the candlestick and upon the left side thereof?

12 And I answered again, and said unto him, What be these two olive branches which through the two golden pipes empty the golden oil out of themselves?

13 And he answered me and said, Knowest thou not what these be? And I said, No, my lord.

14 Then said he, These are the **two anointed ones**, that stand by the Lord of the whole earth.

(KJV)

Now let's focus on Elijah. He lived and had a profound ministry during the reign of kings Ahab and Jehoshaphat. At the end of his ministry as a prophet, he did not die but was translated from earth to heaven by a whirlwind in a chariot of fire.

2 Kings 2:9–13

9 And it came to pass, when they were gone over, that Elijah said unto Elisha, Ask what I shall do for thee, before I be taken away from thee. And Elisha said, I pray thee, let a double portion of thy spirit be upon me.

10 And he said, Thou hast asked a hard thing: nevertheless, if thou see me when I am taken from thee, it shall be so unto thee; but if not, it shall not be so.

11 And it came to pass, as they still went on, and talked, that, behold, there appeared a chariot of fire, and horses of fire, and parted them both asunder; and Elijah went up by a whirlwind into heaven.

12 And Elisha saw it, and he cried, My father, my father, the chariot of Israel, and the horsemen thereof. And he saw him no more: and he took hold of his own clothes, and rent them in two pieces.

13 He took up also the mantle of Elijah that fell from him, and went back, and stood by the bank of Jordan;

(KJV)

So as you can see, Elijah, like Enoch, never saw death, and both were translated to heaven alive. As stated previously, Elijah, along with Moses, appeared to talk to Jesus on the Mount of Transfiguration and would be back to fulfill their ministries during the first half of the tribulation.

Except for these two men, everyone else after the Flood was born, lived their lives, died, and was buried. Their souls/spirits went to Sheol/Hades and remained there until the resurrection of Jesus (for those who were on the Abraham bosom side, also called Paradise). Those on the torment side of Sheol/Hades are still there today. We will see that after the resurrection of Jesus, those on the Paradise side of Sheol/Hades were taken to the third heaven.

Chapter 10

Then There Was Jesus

The cycle of life and death as noted in the previous chapter, besides the exceptions, continued through the Old Testament until we get to Jesus. Jesus is unique in so many ways: His conception, life, and death, and of course, His resurrection.

I will try to keep in sync with the main subject of this book, but I must mention a bit about Jesus.

Jesus's Birth

Jesus was not conceived like any other human. Although His mother, Mary, was human, His Father was divine, God, the Holy Spirit.

Luke 1:26–35

26 And in the sixth month the angel Gabriel was sent from God unto a city of Galilee, named Nazareth,

27 To a virgin espoused to a man whose name was Joseph, of the house of David; and the virgin's name was Mary.

28 And the angel came in unto her, and said, Hail, thou that art highly favoured, the Lord is with thee: blessed art thou among women.

29 And when she saw him, she was troubled at his saying, and cast in her mind what manner of salutation this should be.

30 And the angel said unto her, Fear not, Mary: for thou hast found favour with God.

31 And, behold, thou shalt conceive in thy womb, and bring forth a son, and shalt call his name JESUS.

32 He shall be great, and shall be called the Son of the Highest: and the Lord God shall give unto him the throne of his father David:

33 And he shall reign over the house of Jacob for ever; and of his kingdom there shall be no end.

34 Then said Mary unto the angel, How shall this be, seeing I know not a man?

35 And the angel answered and said unto her, **The Holy Ghost shall come upon thee, and the power of the Highest shall overshadow thee: therefore also that holy thing which shall be born of thee shall be called the Son of God.**

(KJV)

Jesus's Life

Jesus is all God and all Man in the same body, referred to as the hypostatic union. He was not conceived in sin and did not commit any sins. This qualified Him to be Man's Kinsman Redeemer to bridge us back to God through His blood.

Colossians 2:8–9

8 Beware lest any man spoil you through philosophy and vain deceit, after the tradition of men, after the rudiments of the world, and not after Christ.

9 **For in him dwelleth all the fulness of the Godhead bodily**.

(KJV)

Hebrews 4:14–15

14 Seeing then that we have a great high priest, that is passed into the heavens, Jesus the Son of God, let us hold fast our profession.

15 For we have not an high priest which cannot be touched with the feeling of our infirmities; but was in all points tempted like as we are, yet without sin.

(KJV)

Jesus's Death and Burial

Jesus's death is unique. Because He was not born a sinner, since His blood came via the Holy Spirit and not from Joseph, and did not commit any sins, He was not prone to die. He volunteered to die in the place of Man to redeem us back to God through the shedding of His innocent and sinless blood.

Romans 6:23

23 For the wages of sin is death; but the gift of God is eternal life through Jesus Christ our Lord.

(KJV)

John 10:17–18

17 Therefore doth my Father love me, because I lay down my life, that I might take it again.

18 No man taketh it from me, but I lay it down of myself. I have power to lay it down, and I have power to take it again. This commandment have I received of my Father.

(KJV)

Although Jesus did not have to die because He did not inherit the sinful nature of Adam, His death was prophesied in several places in the Old Testament.

Genesis 3:15

15 And I will put enmity between thee and the woman, and between thy seed and her seed; it shall bruise thy head, and thou shalt bruise his heel.

(KJV)

Isaiah 52:13–53:12

13 Behold, my servant shall deal prudently, he shall be exalted and extolled, and be very high.

14 As many were astonied at thee; his visage was so marred more than any man, and his form more than the sons of men:

15 So shall he sprinkle many nations; the kings shall shut their mouths at him: for that which had not been told them shall they see; and that which they had not heard shall they consider.

53 Who hath believed our report? And to whom is the arm of the Lord revealed?

2 For he shall grow up before him as a tender plant, and as a root out of a dry ground: he hath no form nor comeliness; and when we shall see him, there is no beauty that we should desire him.

3 He is despised and rejected of men; a man of sorrows, and acquainted with grief: and we hid as it were our faces from him; he was despised, and we esteemed him not.

4 Surely he hath borne our griefs, and carried our sorrows: yet we did esteem him stricken, smitten of God, and afflicted.

5 But he was wounded for our transgressions, he was bruised for our iniquities: the chastisement of our peace was upon him; and with his stripes we are healed.

6 All we like sheep have gone astray; we have turned every one to his own way; and the Lord hath laid on him the iniquity of us all.

7 He was oppressed, and he was afflicted, yet he opened not his mouth: he is brought as a lamb to the slaugh-

ter, and as a sheep before her shearers is dumb, so he openeth not his mouth.

8 He was taken from prison and from judgment: and who shall declare his generation? For he was cut off out of the land of the living: for the transgression of my people was he stricken.

9 And he made his grave with the wicked, and with the rich in his death; because he had done no violence, neither was any deceit in his mouth.

10 Yet it pleased the Lord to bruise him; he hath put him to grief: when thou shalt make his soul an offering for sin, he shall see his seed, he shall prolong his days, and the pleasure of the Lord shall prosper in his hand.

11 He shall see of the travail of his soul, and shall be satisfied: by his knowledge shall my righteous servant justify many; for he shall bear their iniquities.

12 Therefore will I divide him a portion with the great, and he shall divide the spoil with the strong; **because he hath poured out his soul unto death**: and he was numbered with the transgressors; and he bare the sin of many, and made intercession for the transgressors.

(KJV)

I have listed just a couple of references, but you can also read Psalm 22, Daniel 9:24–26, Zechariah 12:10, and others. The point is that although Jesus died, He did not die just like any other Man. His death was specifically predicted, and at His death, we see the separation of His tripartite being (body, soul, and spirit) that He, along with all other humans, has.

Man was created as a tripartite being with a body, spirit, and soul. The body connects us to the earth, the soul connects us to fellow humans, and our spirit, as created, connects us to God. Upon Adam's sin, our spirit was disconnected from God and could only be reconnected through the blood of Jesus. At the time of physical death, **our soul/spirit** is separated from the body. It is difficult to separate the soul from the spirit, and it can only be separated by the word of God. They always reside together, except for Jesus.

Hebrews 4:12

12 For the word of God is quick, and powerful, and sharper than any two-edged sword, piercing even to the dividing asunder of soul and spirit, and of the joints and marrow, and is a discerner of the thoughts and intents of the heart.

(KJV)

This is why I refer to Man, in death, as separating the body from the soul/spirit. However, with Jesus, we shall see that His body, His soul, and His spirit are all separated at His death. Nowhere else does this appear in the Bible with any other person.

Jesus, on the cross, speaking to one of the thieves, said the following:

Luke 23:39–43

39 And one of the malefactors which were hanged railed on him, saying, If thou be Christ, save thyself and us.

40 But the other answering rebuked him, saying, Dost not thou fear God, seeing thou art in the same condemnation?

41 And we indeed justly; for we receive the due reward of our deeds: but this man hath done nothing amiss.

42 And he said unto Jesus, Lord, remember me when thou comest into thy kingdom.

43 And Jesus said unto him, Verily I say unto thee, To day shalt thou be with me in paradise.

(KJV)

Paradise is where Jesus's soul went upon His death. This is confirmed in Psalm 16.

Psalm 16:9–10

9 Therefore my heart is glad, and my glory rejoiceth: my flesh also shall rest in hope.

10 **For thou wilt not leave my soul in hell**; neither wilt thou suffer thine Holy One to see corruption.

(KJV)

Yet at the moment of His death, Jesus uttered these words:

Luke 23:46

46 And when Jesus had cried with a loud voice, he said, **Father, into thy hands I commend my spirit: and having said thus, he gave up the ghost.**

(KJV)

Finally, after dying at 3:00 p.m., His body was buried in Joseph's new tomb just before 6:00 p.m., the beginning of the first day of the Feast of Unleavened Bread.

Matthew 27:57–60

57 When the even was come, there came a rich man of Arimathaea, named Joseph, who also himself was Jesus' disciple:

58 He went to Pilate, and begged the body of Jesus. Then Pilate commanded the body to be delivered.

59 And when Joseph had taken the body, he wrapped it in a clean linen cloth,

60 And laid it in his own new tomb, which he had hewn out in the rock: and he rolled a great stone to the door of the sepulchre, and departed.

(KJV)

As you saw in the above scriptures, Jesus's **body** was buried in the tomb (grave), His **soul** went to the Paradise side of Sheol/Hades, and His **spirit** was committed to God. This would be His disposition for three days and three nights as He had said in Matthew 12:40.

Matthew 12:40

40 For as Jonas was three days and three nights in the whale's belly; so shall the Son of man be three days and three nights in the heart of the earth.

(KJV)

Jesus's Resurrection

Not only was Jesus's death unique, but also for the first time, a person was resurrected from the dead (Sheol/Hades) in a glorified body. Upon His resurrection, Jesus's glorified body, His Soul, and His

Spirit were reunited in what is referred to as the **prototype body** all humans will have for all eternity. Where this glorified body spends eternity denotes whether you will have eternal life with God or eternal death, forever separated from God.

Colossians 1:12–15

12 Giving thanks unto the Father, which hath made us meet to be partakers of the inheritance of the saints in light:

13 Who hath delivered us from the power of darkness, and hath translated us into the kingdom of his dear Son:

14 In whom we have redemption through his blood, even the forgiveness of sins:

15 Who is the image of the invisible God, the firstborn (Greek – *prototokos* – prototype) of every creature:

(KJV)

After Jesus's resurrection, others were also resurrected in glorified bodies to fulfill the Feast of Firstfruits, as denoted in Leviticus 23.

Matthew 27:50–53

50 Jesus, when he had cried again with a loud voice, yielded up the ghost.

51 And, behold, the veil of the temple was rent in twain from the top to the bottom; and the earth did quake, and the rocks rent;

52 And the graves were opened; and many bodies of the saints which slept arose,

53 And came out of the graves after his resurrection, and went into the holy city, and appeared unto many.

(KJV)

Leviticus 23:10–11

10 Speak unto the children of Israel, and say unto them, **When ye be come into the land which I give unto you, and shall reap the harvest thereof, then ye shall bring a sheaf of the firstfruits of your harvest unto the priest:**

11 And he shall wave the sheaf before the Lord, to be accepted for you: on the morrow after the sabbath the priest shall wave it. (This is the morrow after the weekly sabbath, the first day of the week)

(KJV)

1 Corinthians 15:20–23

20 **But now is Christ risen from the dead, and become the firstfruits of them that slept.**

21 For since by man came death, by man came also the resurrection of the dead.

22 For as in Adam all die, even so in Christ shall all be made alive.

23 But every man in his own order: Christ the firstfruits; afterward they that are Christ's at his coming.

(KJV)

Upon Jesus's resurrection, not only was He the first person resurrected from the grave in a glorified body, but also He moved the location of where the souls/spirits of those who were in the Paradise side of Sheol/Hades would go (in fact, Paradise itself)—to the third heaven. No longer would believers who die in the Lord go **down** to Sheol/Hades, but rather they would go **up** to the third heaven now called Paradise. Praise God, Hallelujah.

Although believers were on the Paradise side of Sheol/Hades before the resurrection of Jesus, they were still held captive. Thank God that Jesus has now also set them and us free.

Ephesians 4:7–10

7 But unto every one of us is given grace according to the measure of the gift of Christ.

8 Wherefore he saith, When he ascended up on high, he led captivity captive (he led a parade of captives – NCV), and gave gifts unto men.

9 (Now that he ascended, what is it but that he also descended first into the lower parts of the earth?

10 He that descended is the same also that ascended up far above all heavens, that he might fill all things.)

(KJV)

2 Corinthians 12:1–4

1 It is not expedient for me doubtless to glory. I will come to visions and revelations of the Lord.

2 I knew a man in Christ above fourteen years ago, (whether in the body, I cannot tell; or whether out of the body, I

cannot tell: God knoweth**;) such an one caught up to the third heaven.**

3 And I knew such a man, (whether in the body, or out of the body, I cannot tell: God knoweth;)

4 How that he was caught up into paradise, and heard unspeakable words, which it is not lawful for a man to utter.

(KJV)

So now, after the resurrection of Jesus, the bodies of both the saved and the unsaved still go to the grave. The souls/spirits of the unsaved still go to Sheol/Hades, which, at this time, only consists of the torment side.

But the souls/spirits of the saved go immediately to the third heaven called Paradise. Paul confirms this.

2 Corinthians 5:6–9

6 Therefore we are always confident, knowing that, **whilst we are at home in the body, we are absent from the Lord:**

7 (For we walk by faith, not by sight:)

8 We are confident, I say, and willing rather **to be absent from the body, and to be present with the Lord.**

9 Wherefore we labour, that, whether present or absent, we may be accepted of him.

(KJV)

Philippians 1:19–23

19 For I know that this shall turn to my salvation through your prayer, and the supply of the Spirit of Jesus Christ,

20 According to my earnest expectation and my hope, that in nothing I shall be ashamed, but that with all boldness, as always, so now also Christ shall be magnified in my body, whether it be by life, or by death.

21 For to me to live is Christ, and to die is gain.

22 But if I live in the flesh, this is the fruit of my labour: yet what I shall choose I wot not.

23 For I am in a strait betwixt two, having a desire to depart, and to be with Christ; which is far better:

(KJV)

Before I end this chapter, please note that the decision you make about Jesus in time, whether to accept Him as your Lord and Savior or to reject Him, determines where you go immediately after death and through all eternity. Now is the time to confess that you are a sinner who needs a Savior (Jesus), repent your sins, and be baptized in obedience to the Lord's command. A second after physical death is too late. As I was once told, "Hell will be a realization realized too late."

Technology, politics, philosophy, logic, knowledge, pedigrees, and wealth will **not** save you. Only the precious blood of Jesus Christ that He shed for all people, when applied to you, will save you.

1 Peter 1:18–23

18 Forasmuch as ye know that ye were not redeemed with corruptible things, as silver and gold, from your

vain conversation received by tradition from your
fathers;

**19 But with the precious blood of Christ, as of a lamb
without blemish and without spot:**

20 Who verily was foreordained before the foundation of
the world, but was manifest in these last times for you,

**21 Who by him do believe in God, that raised him up
from the dead, and gave him glory; that your faith and
hope might be in God.**

22 Seeing ye have purified your souls in obeying the truth
through the Spirit unto unfeigned love of the brethren, see
that ye love one another with a pure heart fervently:

**23 Being born again, not of corruptible seed, but of
incorruptible, by the word of God, which liveth and
abideth for ever.**

(KJV)

Chapter 11

Heaven

Up to this point in the book, we have been talking about the Grave, Sheol/Hades, and Paradise, but not a deep focus is given on heaven. Well, now we will focus on heaven and its inhabitants over time.

It is wise to recall the Bible makes clear that before there was anything created, there was God and only God. There was no heaven, no universe, no earth, no angels, no creature of any kind. It may be difficult for us to imagine that, but that is precisely what the Bible says.

John 1:1–2

> 1 In the beginning was the Word, and the Word was with God, and the Word was God.

> 2 The same was in the beginning with God.

> (KJV)

The beginning referred to in John 1:1 is before the creation of any and all things.

It has been asked, if nothing had been created in John 1:1, where was God? It is great to know that the Bible answers this question in the following verse:

Isaiah 57:15

15 For thus saith the high and lofty One that **inhabiteth eternity**, whose name is Holy;

(KJV)

Our human minds cannot comprehend eternity. We are beings of time, which is merely a subset of eternity. Before there was a when, where, then, or there, there was only God who inhabited eternity.

So, in Genesis 1:1, we are told about the creation of space, time, and matter. All these must come into being at the same time. Matter must have space to exist. Space with no matter is meaningless. Matter and Space without time are static and useless.

Genesis 1:1

1 In the beginning God created the Heaven and the earth.

(KJV)

Although it does not clearly show itself in the (KJV) Bible, most modern translations do reflect the word "heaven" is in the plural tense. In Hebrew, it is the word *shamayim*, which is in the dual Hebrew tense. Not the singular tense (for one) or the plural tense (for three or more), but rather in the Hebrew dual tense (for two).

Paul tells us in 2 Corinthians 12 that there are three heavens, and the third heaven is where God dwells.

2 Corinthians 12:2

2 I knew a man in Christ above fourteen years ago, (whether in the body, I cannot tell; or whether out of the body, I cannot tell: God knoweth;) such an one caught up to the third heaven.

(KJV)

Since there are three heavens, why does Genesis 1:1 refer to heaven in the dual tense? This is answered in Genesis 1:6–8, which occurred on the second day of creation.

Genesis 1:6–8

6 And God said, Let there be a firmament in the midst of the waters, and let it divide the waters from the waters.

7 And God made the firmament, and divided the waters which were under the firmament from the waters which were above the firmament: and it was so.

8 **And God called the firmament Heaven**. And the evening and the morning were the second day.

(KJV)

Now we have three heavens.

The first heaven is what we call today the atmosphere around the earth (the firmament), the second heaven is what we call the universe, and the third heaven is where God currently exists.

Now let's roll time back to the first day of creation. God, who inhabited eternity in the eternal realm, began to reside in the third heaven in the realm of time. He created the second heaven to contain all the billions of galaxies, stars, and planets that would be for the pinnacle of His creation on the sixth day, Man, to enjoy and observe. God didn't need any of this to exist but rather created it for Man.

Please note that initially, the first and only person to inhabit the third heaven was God and God alone. There were no angels, and certainly there was no Man. It is believed the angels were created somewhere between Day 1 and Day 2 since the earth was not physically formed until Day 3. The heavens and the earth were created on Day 1, but the earth was not physically formed until Day 3. Job indicates the angels were here to witness the forming of the earth.

Genesis 1:1–13

1 In the beginning God created the Heaven and the earth.

2 And the earth was without form, and void; and darkness was upon the face of the deep. And the Spirit of God moved upon the face of the waters.

3 And God said, Let there be light: and there was light.

4 And God saw the light, that it was good: and God divided the light from the darkness.

5 And God called the light Day, and the darkness he called Night. And the evening and the morning were the **first day**.

6 And God said, Let there be a firmament in the midst of the waters, and let it divide the waters from the waters.

7 And God made the firmament, and divided the waters which were under the firmament from the waters which were above the firmament: and it was so.

8 And God called the firmament Heaven. And the evening and the morning were the **second day.**

9 And God said, Let the waters under the heaven be gathered together unto one place, and let the dry land appear: and it was so.

10 And God called **the dry land Earth**; and the gathering together of the waters called the Seas: and God saw that it was good.

11 And God said, Let the earth bring forth grass, the herb yielding seed, and the fruit tree yielding fruit after his kind, whose seed is in itself, upon the earth: and it was so.

12 And the earth brought forth grass, and herb yielding seed after his kind, and the tree yielding fruit, whose seed was in itself, after his kind: and God saw that it was good.

13 And the evening and the morning were the **third day**.

(KJV)

Job 38:4–7

4 **Where wast thou when I laid the foundations of the earth?** declare, if thou hast understanding.

5 Who hath laid the measures thereof, if thou knowest? or who hath stretched the line upon it?

6 Whereupon are the foundations thereof fastened? or who laid the corner stone thereof;

7 **When the morning stars sang together, and all the sons of God shouted for joy?**

(KJV)

With all this in mind, as we consider the time element, God, at the beginning, inhabited the third heaven alone. By the time the earth was formed on Day 3 of creation, angels also inhabited the third heaven, where they can still reside today. They were the only beings inhabiting the third heaven until God translated Enoch to heaven in Genesis 5 and Hebrews 11:

Genesis 5:18–24

18 And Jared lived an hundred sixty and two years, and he begat Enoch:

19 And Jared lived after he begat Enoch eight hundred years, and begat sons and daughters:

20 And all the days of Jared were nine hundred sixty and two years: and he died.

21 And Enoch lived sixty and five years, and begat Methuselah:

22 And Enoch walked with God after he begat Methuselah three hundred years, and begat sons and daughters:

23 And all the days of Enoch were three hundred sixty and five years:

24 And Enoch walked with God: and he was not; for God took him.

(KJV)

Hebrews 11:5

5 By faith Enoch was translated that he should not see death; and was not found, because God had translated him: for before his translation he had this testimony, that he pleased God.

(KJV)

Enoch became the first human to inhabit the third heaven. This would remain that way until Moses and Elijah were translated there as well. *See my references to Moses and Elijah in Chapter 7.* All other believers up to the resurrection of Jesus went to Sheol/Hades on the Paradise side. In fact, that is where Jesus went upon His death on the cross.

The great news is that after Jesus's resurrection, Paradise and all the inhabitants thereof were transferred to the third heaven that is now also called Paradise, or as Jesus referred to it, His "Father's House." However, only their souls/spirits are there. Their bodies are still in the grave.

John 14:1–3

14 Let not your heart be troubled: ye believe in God, believe also in me.

2 In **my Father's house** are many mansions: if it were not so, I would have told you. I go to prepare a place for you.

3 And if I go and prepare a place for you, I will come again, and receive you unto myself; that where I am, there ye may be also.

(KJV)

Now please note that Jesus was describing the third heaven as it exists today as His Father's House with many mansions (room.) If you notice, Jesus said He was going **to prepare a place** for believers, which cannot be the third heaven as we know it today.

Heaven, as it exists today, is not described in detail in the Bible. We know that God is there, some of the angels are there, Enoch, Moses, and Elijah are there in their bodies, but all other believers (Old Testament and New Testament) are there as soul/spirit beings, with their bodies still in the grave.

Revelation Chapter 4 describes the third heaven **after the Rapture of the Church** when those who are members of the body of Christ had died and have been raised from the grave in their glorified bodies and reunited with their souls/spirits that Jesus is going to bring **with** Him from the third heaven. Believers who are still alive at the Rapture will have their bodies changed from mortal to glorified bodies, and we will all go back to the third heaven with Jesus.

1 Thessalonians 4:13–18

13 But I would not have you to be ignorant, brethren, concerning them which are asleep, that ye sorrow not, even as others which have no hope.

14 For if we believe that Jesus died and rose again**, even so them also which sleep in Jesus will God bring with him.**

15 For this we say unto you by the word of the Lord, that we which are alive and remain unto the coming of the Lord shall not prevent them which are asleep.

16 For the Lord himself shall descend from heaven with a shout, with the voice of the archangel, and with the trump of God: **and the dead in Christ shall rise first**:

17 Then we which are alive and remain shall be caught up together with them in the clouds, to meet the Lord in the air: and so shall we ever be with the Lord.

18 Wherefore comfort one another with these words.

(KJV)

1 Corinthians 15:42–55

42 So also is the resurrection of the dead. It is sown in corruption; it is raised in incorruption:

43 It is sown in dishonour; it is raised in glory: it is sown in weakness; it is raised in power:

44 It is sown a natural body; it is raised a spiritual body. There is a natural body, and there is a spiritual body.

45 And so it is written, The first man Adam was made a living soul; the last Adam was made a quickening spirit.

46 Howbeit that was not first which is spiritual, but that which is natural; and afterward that which is spiritual.

47 The first man is of the earth, earthy: the second man is the Lord from heaven.

48 As is the earthy, such are they also that are earthy: and as is the heavenly, such are they also that are heavenly.

49 And as we have borne the image of the earthy, we shall also bear the image of the heavenly.

50 Now this I say, brethren, that flesh and blood cannot inherit the kingdom of God; neither doth corruption inherit incorruption.

51 Behold, I shew you a mystery; We shall not all sleep, but we shall all be changed,

52 In a moment, in the twinkling of an eye, at the last trump: for the trumpet shall sound, and the dead shall be raised incorruptible, and we shall be changed.

53 For this corruptible must put on incorruption, and this mortal must put on immortality.

54 So when this corruptible shall have put on incorruption, and this mortal shall have put on immortality, then shall be brought to pass the saying that is written, Death is swallowed up in victory.

55 O death, where is thy sting? O grave, where is thy victory?

(KJV)

It is after the body of Christ has been raptured to the third heaven and gone through the Judgment Seat of Christ to receive our rewards/ inheritance that Revelation Chapter 4 begins to describe the third heaven.

The Judgment Seat of Christ (For Believers in the Body of Christ Only)

2 Corinthians 5:1–10

1 For we know that if our earthly house of this tabernacle were dissolved, we have a building of God, a house not made with hands, eternal in the heavens.

2 For in this we groan, earnestly desiring to be clothed upon with our house which is from heaven:

3 If so be that being clothed we shall not be found naked.

4 For we that are in this tabernacle do groan, being burdened: not for that we would be unclothed, but clothed upon, that mortality might be swallowed up of life.

5 Now he that hath wrought us for the selfsame thing is God, who also hath given unto us the earnest of the Spirit.

6 Therefore we are always confident, knowing that, whilst we are at home in the body, we are absent from the Lord:

7 (For we walk by faith, not by sight:)

8 We are confident, I say, and willing rather to be absent from the body, and to be present with the Lord.

9 Wherefore we labour, that, whether present or absent, we may be accepted of him.

10 For we must all appear before **the judgment seat of Christ**; that every one may receive the things done in his body, according to that he hath done, whether it be good or bad.

(KJV)

1 Corinthians 3:9–15

9 For we are labourers together with God: ye are God's husbandry, ye are God's building.

10 According to the grace of God which is given unto me, as a wise masterbuilder, I have laid the foundation, and another buildeth thereon. But let every man take heed how he buildeth thereupon.

11 For other foundation can no man lay than that is laid, which is Jesus Christ.

12 Now if any man build upon this foundation gold, silver, precious stones, wood, hay, stubble;

13 Every man's work shall be made manifest: for the day shall declare it, because it shall be revealed by fire; and the fire shall try every man's work of what sort it is.

14 If any man's work abide which he hath built thereupon, he shall receive a reward.

15 If any man's work shall be burned, he shall suffer loss: but he himself shall be saved; yet so as by fire.

(KJV)

Romans 14:7–10

7 For none of us liveth to himself, and no man dieth to himself.

8 For whether we live, we live unto the Lord; and whether we die, we die unto the Lord: whether we live therefore, or die, we are the Lord's.

9 For to this end Christ both died, and rose, and revived, that he might be Lord both of the dead and living.

10 But why dost thou judge thy brother? or why dost thou set at nought thy brother? for we shall all stand before **the judgment seat of Christ**.

(KJV)

The Third Heaven Described in Revelation 4 (After the Rapture of the Body of Christ [the Church])

Revelation 4

4 After this I looked, and, behold, a door was opened in heaven: and the first voice which I heard was as it were of a trumpet talking with me; which said, Come up hither, and I will shew thee things which must be hereafter.

2 And immediately I was in the spirit: and, behold, **a throne was set in heaven, and one sat on the throne.**

3 And he that sat was to look upon like a jasper and a sardine stone: and there was a rainbow round about the throne, in sight like unto an emerald.

4 And round about the throne were four and twenty seats: and upon the seats I saw four and twenty elders sitting, clothed in white raiment; and they had on their heads crowns of gold.

5 And out of the throne proceeded lightnings and thunderings and voices: **and there were seven lamps of fire burning before the throne, which are the seven Spirits of God.**

6 **And before the throne there was a sea of glass like unto crystal: and in the midst of the throne, and round about the throne, were four beasts full of eyes before and behind.**

7 And the first beast was like a lion, and the second beast like a calf, and the third beast had a face as a man, and the fourth beast was like a flying eagle.

8 And the four beasts had each of them six wings about him; and they were full of eyes within: and they rest not day and night, saying, Holy, holy, holy, Lord God Almighty, which was, and is, and is to come.

9 And when those beasts give glory and honour and thanks to him that sat on the throne, who liveth for ever and ever,

10 The four and twenty elders fall down before him that sat on the throne, and worship him that liveth for ever and ever, and cast their crowns before the throne, saying,

11 Thou art worthy, O Lord, to receive glory and honour and power: for thou hast created all things, and for thy pleasure they are and were created.

(KJV)

Revelation 5:1–6

5 And I saw in the right hand of him that sat on the throne a book written within and on the backside, sealed with seven seals.

2 And I saw a strong angel proclaiming with a loud voice, Who is worthy to open the book, and to loose the seals thereof?

3 And no man in heaven, nor in earth, neither under the earth, was able to open the book, neither to look thereon.

4 And I wept much, because no man was found worthy to open and to read the book, neither to look thereon.

5 And one of the elders saith unto me, Weep not: behold, the Lion of the tribe of Juda, the Root of David, hath prevailed to open the book, and to loose the seven seals thereof.

6 And I beheld, and, lo, in the midst of the throne and of the four beasts, and in the midst of the elders, stood a Lamb as it had been slain, having seven horns and seven eyes, which are the seven Spirits of God sent forth into all the earth.

(KJV)

At this time, the third heaven is populated with God (including Jesus as a Lamb as it had been slain and the Holy Spirit as the seven Spirits of God), the angels (including Satan and the one-third that follow him), three men in their human bodies (Enoch, Moses, and Elijah), all the members of the body of Christ in their glorified bodies (the 24 elders and the sea of glass like unto crystal), and the Old Testament Saints still in their soul/spirit bodies.

The Old Testament Saints who were not raised as part of the Firstfruits upon Jesus's resurrection are still in the souls/spirits under the altar in the third heaven. They will be joined by the souls/spirits of believers who die during the Tribulation (Tribulation Saints).

Revelation 6:9–11

9 And when he had opened the fifth seal, I saw **under the altar** the souls of them that were slain for the word of God, and for the testimony which they held:

10 And they cried with a loud voice, saying, How long, O Lord, holy and true, dost thou not judge and avenge our blood on them that dwell on the earth?

11 And white robes were given unto every one of them; and it was said unto them, that they should rest yet for a little season, until their fellowservants also and their brethren, that should be killed as they were, should be fulfilled.

(KJV)

Throughout the Tribulation, the souls/spirits of believers who die will be placed under the altar in the third heaven, which is still called Paradise, since this is after the resurrection of Jesus from the grave.

At the beginning of the Tribulation, Moses and Elijah will be transported to earth in **human bodies** for a three-and-a-half-year ministry to the Jews, being stationed in Jerusalem. At the end of their earthly ministry, they both will be killed but, after three and a half days, will be resurrected from the dead, given **glorified bodies**, and caught back up into the third heaven.

Revelation 11:3–12

3 And I will give power unto my two witnesses, and they shall prophesy a thousand two hundred and threescore days, clothed in sackcloth.

4 These are the two olive trees, and the two candlesticks standing before the God of the earth.

5 And if any man will hurt them, fire proceedeth out of their mouth, and devoureth their enemies: and if any man will hurt them, he must in this manner be killed.

6 These have power to shut heaven, that it rain not in the days of their prophecy: and have power over waters to turn them to blood, and to smite the earth with all plagues, as often as they will.

7 And when they shall have finished their testimony, the beast that ascendeth out of the bottomless pit shall make war against them, and shall overcome them, and kill them.

8 And their dead bodies shall lie in the street of the great city, which spiritually is called Sodom and Egypt, where also our Lord was crucified.

9 And they of the people and kindreds and tongues and nations shall see their dead bodies three days and an half, and shall not suffer their dead bodies to be put in graves.

10 And they that dwell upon the earth shall rejoice over them, and make merry, and shall send gifts one to another; because these two prophets tormented them that dwelt on the earth.

11 And after three days and an half the Spirit of life from God entered into them, and they stood upon their feet; and great fear fell upon them which saw them.

12 And they heard a great voice from heaven saying unto them, Come up hither. And they ascended up to heaven in a cloud; and their enemies beheld them.

(KJV)

It should also be noted that at the beginning of the **Great Tribulation**, Satan and all the angels who sided with him (one-third of the angels created) will be cast out of the third and second heaven and will be limited to earth and earth alone. This will be another change in the inhabitants of the third heaven over time.

The status of the third heaven, without Satan and his angels, will remain the same until the end of the Great Tribulation when there will be the resurrection of the Old Testament Saints (Israel and others that believed God) and the Tribulation Saints. They will be given glorified bodies, just as the Church, and go through their judgment.

Revelation 20:1–5

1 And I saw an angel come down from heaven, having the key of the bottomless pit and a great chain in his hand.

2 And he laid hold on the dragon, that old serpent, which is the Devil, and Satan, and bound him a thousand years,

3 And cast him into the bottomless pit, and shut him up, and set a seal upon him, that he should deceive the nations no more, till the thousand years should be fulfilled: and after that he must be loosed a little season.

4 And I saw thrones, and they sat upon them, and judgment was given unto them: and I saw the souls of them that were beheaded for the witness of Jesus, and for the word of God, and which had not worshipped the beast, neither his image, neither had received his mark upon their foreheads, or in their hands; and they lived and reigned with Christ a thousand years.

5 But the rest of the dead lived not again until the thousand years were finished. This is the first resurrection.

(KJV)

Daniel 12:1–2

12 And at that time shall Michael stand up, the great prince which standeth for the children of thy people: and there shall be a time of trouble, such as never was since there was a nation even to that same time: **and at that time thy people shall be delivered, every one that shall be found written in the book.**

2 And many of them that sleep in the dust of the earth shall awake, some to everlasting life, and some to shame and everlasting contempt.

(KJV)

The status of the third heaven will remain the same throughout the Millennium, the one-thousand-year reign of Christ on the earth as prophesied, but will change again before we enter eternity with God. I will deal with this in the next chapter.

Chapter 12

The Final States

In this chapter, we will deal with the final states of heaven, the earth, Sheol/Hades, and Gehenna (the Lake of Fire). This will be the culmination of seven thousand years of history per the Bible.

At the beginning of Revelation Chapter 20, Satan, the fallen angels, unclean spirits, and demons will be cast into the Abyss (the bottomless pit) for one thousand years and thus will have no interaction or influence with anyone on earth or in heaven. Praise God.

Revelation 20:1–3

20 And I saw an angel come down from heaven, having the key of the bottomless pit and a great chain in his hand.

2 And he laid hold on the dragon, that old serpent, which is the Devil, and Satan, and bound him a thousand years,

3 And cast him into the bottomless pit, and shut him up, and set a seal upon him, that he should deceive the nations no more, till the thousand years should be fulfilled: and after that he must be loosed a little season.

(KJV)

Immediately after this, the Old Testament Saints, including Israel, and all the Tribulation Saints will be resurrected and given their glorified bodies and will receive their judgment. They, along with the Church (the Bride of Christ), will enter the Millennium Kingdom in their glorified bodies and will reign with Christ on earth.

Per Matthew 26 those few who survive the Tribulation period in their natural bodies will be judged by Jesus before they will be allowed to enter the Millennium Kingdom. Those who helped His brethren (the Jews) during the Tribulation will accept Jesus as Lord and Savior and thus will be allowed to enter the Millennium Kingdom in their natural bodies.

Those who did not help His brethren during the tribulation will be cast into everlasting punishment, beginning in Sheol/Hades and continuing in the lake of fire at the end of the Millennium following the Great White Throne Judgment.

Matthew 25:31–46

31 When the Son of man shall come in his glory, and all the holy angels with him, then shall he sit upon the throne of his glory:

32 And before him shall be gathered all nations: and he shall separate them one from another, as a shepherd divideth his sheep from the goats:

33 And he shall set the sheep on his right hand, but the goats on the left.

34 Then shall the King say unto them on his right hand, Come, ye blessed of my Father, inherit the kingdom prepared for you from the foundation of the world:

35 For I was an hungred, and ye gave me meat: I was thirsty, and ye gave me drink: I was a stranger, and ye took me in:

36 Naked, and ye clothed me: I was sick, and ye visited me: I was in prison, and ye came unto me.

37 Then shall the righteous answer him, saying, Lord, when saw we thee an hungred, and fed thee? or thirsty, and gave thee drink?

38 When saw we thee a stranger, and took thee in? or naked, and clothed thee?

39 Or when saw we thee sick, or in prison, and came unto thee?

40 And the King shall answer and say unto them, Verily I say unto you, Inasmuch as ye have done it unto one of the least of these my brethren, ye have done it unto me.

41 Then shall he say also unto them on the left hand, Depart from me, ye cursed, into everlasting fire, prepared for the devil and his angels:

42 For I was an hungred, and ye gave me no meat: I was thirsty, and ye gave me no drink:

43 I was a stranger, and ye took me not in: naked, and ye clothed me not: sick, and in prison, and ye visited me not.

44 Then shall they also answer him, saying, Lord, when saw we thee an hungred, or athirst, or a stranger, or naked, or sick, or in prison, and did not minister unto thee?

45 Then shall he answer them, saying, Verily I say unto you, Inasmuch as ye did it not to one of the least of these, ye did it not to me.

46 And these shall go away into everlasting punishment: but the righteous into life eternal.

(KJV)

The Millennium Kingdom

The Millennium Kingdom will start with Jesus as King of the earth, those in glorified bodies (the Church, Old Testament Saints, Tribulation Saints) reigning with Him, and those in natural bodies repopulating the earth during one thousand years of peace. Can you imagine that?

However, in these one thousand years of peace, those in their natural bodies will have children, and they will have children, and the cycle continues for one thousand years. Those who initially entered the Kingdom in their natural bodies had accepted Jesus as Lord and Savior. Since salvation requires a personal decision about Jesus, each child born during that time frame will have to make a personal decision regarding accepting Christ. Not just through compliance with the millennium rules, but with their heart.

Romans 10:9–10

9 That if thou shalt confess with thy mouth the Lord Jesus, and shalt believe in thine heart that God hath raised him from the dead, thou shalt be saved.

10 For with the heart man believeth unto righteousness; and with the mouth confession is made unto salvation.

(KJV)

Unfortunately, during the millennium, there will be individuals who will **not** accept Jesus as their Lord and Savior, though He will be their King. They will do lip service but not accept Jesus in their hearts. This is sad, though it will be true.

At the end of the one-thousand-year reign of Jesus on earth, Satan and all his cohorts will be released from the bottomless pit and go throughout the earth and deceive those (in their natural bodies) who had not accepted Jesus as their Lord and Savior. Together, they will put forth an effort to dethrone the King of Kings and Lord of Lords.

Their efforts will fail by the intervention of God, the Father in heaven. He will reign down fire from heaven to destroy all who were against Jesus in their natural bodies and will cast Satan and all his cohorts into the lake of fire.

Though it is not directly stated, based on previous examples, those who were in their natural bodies and had accepted Jesus as Lord and Savior will be given glorified bodies and experience judgment for their inheritance and rewards like all the previous groups.

That leaves everyone in the spiritual realm (God, the Angels, and Man, whether saved or condemned).

Revelation 20:7–10

7 And when the thousand years are expired, Satan shall be loosed out of his prison,

8 And shall go out to deceive the nations which are in the four quarters of the earth, Gog and Magog, to gather them

together to battle: the number of whom is as the sand of the sea.

9 And they went up on the breadth of the earth, and compassed the camp of the saints about, and the beloved city: and fire came down from God out of heaven, and devoured them.

10 And the devil that deceived them was cast into the lake of fire and brimstone, where the beast and the false prophet are, and shall be tormented day and night for ever and ever.

(KJV)

As you noticed, the lake of fire increased its inhabitants with Satan, the one-third of the angels who aligned with him, and all evil spirits and demonic beings. The beast and the false prophet had spent the entire millennium period there. They finally received some company.

The Great White Throne Judgment

At the Great White Throne Judgment, heaven and earth will pass away, and all who rejected God's way of salvation (whose names were not written in the Book of Life) will be brought before the throne, fairly judged according to their works, and immediately cast into the lake of fire and brimstone. As you can see, the lake of fire population will be increased as a result of this judgment. Even death and Sheol/Hades, including Tartarus, will be cast into the lake of fire.

Revelation 20:11–15

11 And I saw a great white throne, and him that sat on it, from whose face the earth and the heaven fled away; and there was found no place for them.

12 And I saw the dead, small and great, stand before God; and the books were opened: and another book was opened, which is the book of life: and the dead were judged out of those things which were written in the books, according to their works.

13 And the sea gave up the dead which were in it; and death and hell delivered up the dead which were in them: and they were judged every man according to their works.

14 And death and hell were cast into the lake of fire. This is the second death.

15 And whosoever was not found written in the book of life was cast into the lake of fire.

(KJV)

A New Heaven and a New Earth

After the Great White Throne Judgment, all evil will reside in the lake of fire, and the redeemed, all in glorified bodies, will receive their new home—a new heaven and a new earth.

The new earth will be different in that there will be no more sea. Remember, spiritual (glorified) bodies don't need physical food, water, rest, etc. We will simply live forever with bodies like Christ.

1 John 3:2

2 Beloved, now are we the sons of God, and it doth not yet appear what we shall be: but we know that, when he shall appear, **we shall be like him**; for we shall see him as he is.

(KJV)

The new heaven will be different from the one that currently exists. Jesus talked about the current heaven in John 14. It is also described in the Book of Revelation in Chapters 4 and 5 and throughout the book until Chapter 21 when we receive a new heaven and a new earth.

The current heaven is referred to as "My Father's House" in John 14, but Jesus said He was going to prepare a place for us, the new heaven that we see in Revelation 21.

As you noticed, the current heaven described in Revelation 4 and 5 has no mention of streets of gold, twelve gates, or twelve foundations. Those are attributes of the new heaven that Jesus is preparing for us. I know this may disappoint some believers, but the good news is one day, you will indeed walk streets of gold, but maybe not at this time. I believe the better way to see it all is that no matter what, you will be with Jesus.

John 14:1–3

14 Let not your heart be troubled: ye believe in God, believe also in me.

2 **In my Father's house are many mansions (rooms):** if it were not so, I would have told you. **I go to prepare a place for you.**

3 And if I go and prepare a place for you, I will come again, and receive you unto myself; that where I am, there ye may be also.

(KJV)

Now let's look at the attributes of the new and eternal heaven as recorded in Revelation 21.

Revelation 21:10–27

10 And he carried me away in the spirit to a great and high mountain, and shewed me that great city, **the holy Jerusalem, descending out of heaven from God,**

11 Having the glory of God: and her light was like unto a stone most precious, even like a jasper stone, clear as crystal;

12 And had a wall great and high, and had **twelve gates**, and at the gates twelve angels, and names written thereon, which are the names of the twelve tribes of the children of Israel:

13 On the east three gates; on the north three gates; on the south three gates; and on the west three gates.

14 And the wall of the city had **twelve foundations**, and in them the names of the twelve apostles of the Lamb.

15 And he that talked with me had a golden reed to measure the city, and the gates thereof, and the wall thereof.

16 And the city lieth foursquare, and the length is as large as the breadth: and he measured the city with the reed, twelve thousand furlongs. The length and the breadth and the height of it are equal.

17 And he measured the wall thereof, an hundred and forty and four cubits, according to the measure of a man, that is, of the angel.

18 And the building of the wall of it was of jasper: and the city was pure gold, like unto clear glass.

19 And the foundations of the wall of the city were garnished with all manner of precious stones. The first foundation was jasper; the second, sapphire; the third, a chalcedony; the fourth, an emerald;

20 The fifth, sardonyx; the sixth, sardius; the seventh, chrysolite; the eighth, beryl; the ninth, a topaz; the tenth, a chrysoprasus; the eleventh, a jacinth; the twelfth, an amethyst.

21 And the twelve gates were twelve pearls; every several gate was of one pearl: and the street of the city was pure gold, as it were transparent glass.

22 And I saw **no temple therein**: for the Lord God Almighty and the Lamb are the temple of it.

23 And the city had no need of the sun, neither of the moon, to shine in it: for the glory of God did lighten it, and the Lamb is the light thereof.

24 And the nations of them which are saved shall walk in the light of it: and the kings of the earth do bring their glory and honour into it.

25 And the gates of it shall not be shut at all by day: for there shall be no night there.

26 And they shall bring the glory and honour of the nations into it.

27 And there shall in no wise enter into it any thing that defileth, neither whatsoever worketh abomination, or

maketh a lie: but they which are written in the Lamb's book of life.

(KJV)

Revelation 22:1–5

22 And he shewed me a pure river of water of life, clear as crystal, proceeding out of the throne of God and of the Lamb.

2 In the midst of the street of it, and on either side of the river, was there the tree of life, which bare twelve manner of fruits, and yielded her fruit every month: and the leaves of the tree were for the healing of the nations.

3 And there shall be no more curse: but the throne of God and of the Lamb shall be in it; and his servants shall serve him:

4 And they shall see his face; and his name shall be in their foreheads.

5 And there shall be no night there; and they need no candle, neither light of the sun; for the Lord God giveth them light: and they shall reign for ever and ever.

(KJV)

Summing It All Up

So as eternity begins for us (the redeemed),

- All evil and its participants, including Satan, will exist in the **eternal** lake of fire, tormented forever and ever.

- ○ Death and hell will be there.
- ○ Sheol/Hades and the Grave will be there.
- ○ Tartarus and the Bottomless Pit will be there.
- All Good, from God to the angels and believers in their glorified bodies, will have access to the new heaven, the new earth, and the entire universe.

  - ○ **The Triune God will be there:**

Revelation 22:1

22 And he shewed me a pure river of water of life **(The Holy Spirit)**, clear as crystal, proceeding out of the throne of God **(The Father)** and of the Lamb **(Jesus, God, the Son)**.

(KJV)

John 7:37–39

37 In the last day, that great day of the feast, Jesus stood and cried, saying, If any man thirst, let him come unto me, and drink.

38 He that believeth on me, as the scripture hath said, **out of his belly shall flow rivers of living water.**

39 (But this spake he of the Spirit, which they that believe on him should receive: for the Holy Ghost was not yet given; because that Jesus was not yet glorified.)

(KJV)

○　**The Tree of Life will be there:**

Revelation 22:2

2 In the midst of the street of it, and on either side of the river, was there **the tree of life**, which bare twelve manner of fruits, and yielded her fruit every month: and the leaves of the tree were for the healing of the nations.

(KJV)

○　**We, His Servants (Angels and Man), will be there:**

Revelation 22:3–5

3 And there shall be no more curse: but the throne of God and of the Lamb shall be in it; **and his servants shall serve him**:

4 And they shall see his face; and his name shall be in their foreheads.

5 And there shall be no night there; and they need no candle, neither light of the sun; for the Lord God giveth them light: and they shall reign for ever and ever.

(KJV)

As you can see in the end, good wins, and evil is set apart. Though it will take thousands of years, God will have things like He originally created them to be, all in alignment with Him, for we were created for His good pleasure.

Revelation 4:11

11 Thou art worthy, O Lord, to receive glory and honour and power: **for thou hast created all things, and for thy pleasure they are and were created.**

(KJV)

In the meantime, we should be praying as it says in the Model Prayer and Last Prayer in the Bible:

Matthew 6:9–10

9 After this manner therefore pray ye: Our Father which art in heaven, Hallowed be thy name.

10 **Thy kingdom come. Thy will be done in earth, as it is in heaven.**

(KJV)

Revelation 22:20

Even so, come, Lord Jesus

(KJV)

Revelation 22:21

21 The grace of our Lord Jesus Christ be with you all. Amen.

(KJV)

Chapter 13

Epilogue

I pray that after reading this book, you can see that all the places God created in the first six days

1) were real and
2) had a purpose (whether temporary or permanent), and
3) their occupants changed over time, and
4) they will all culminate either in the new heaven and earth or the eternal lake of fire.

My prayer is that you accept Jesus Christ as your personal Lord and Savior while you are in your natural body. After you leave your natural body, your eternal destination is permanently set. Please remember that we are all eternal beings who are currently housed in a natural body. You will exist eternally somewhere (with God or in the Lake of Fire). The decision is yours, and I pray that it is for Jesus.

If you are already saved, I pray this book has helped you see how things change over time.

If you are not saved, I pray that you do so before it is too late. Below is a simple plan of salvation. If you are serious and follow it, I will see you in heaven.

2 Corinthians 13:14

14 The grace of the Lord Jesus Christ, and the love of God, and the communion of the Holy Ghost, be with you all. Amen.

(KJV)

Chapter 14

Plan of Salvation

(How to Be Saved)

1. **We must admit that we are all sinners, both by birth and by behavior**

   Romans 3:23
   23 For all have sinned, and come short of the glory of God;
   (KJV)

   Romans 3:10
   10 As it is written, There is none righteous, no, not one:
   (KJV)

2. **We must recognize that sin carries a wage—Death (spiritual separation from God).**

   Romans 6:23
   23 For the wages of sin is death; but the gift of God is eternal life through Jesus Christ our Lord
   (KJV)

Romans 5:12

12 Wherefore, as by one man sin entered into the world, and death by sin; and so death passed upon all men, for that all have sinned:

(KJV)

3. **However, we can rejoice because God has provided a Substitute to die in our stead—Jesus.**

Romans 5:8

8 But God commendeth his love toward us, in that, while we were yet sinners, Christ died for us.

(KJV)

John 3:16–18

16 For God so loved the world, that he gave his only begotten Son, that whosoever believeth in him should not perish, but have everlasting life.
17 For God sent not his Son into the world to condemn the world; but that the world through him might be saved.
18 He that believeth on him is not condemned: but he that believeth not is condemned already, because he hath not believed in the name of the only begotten Son of God.

(KJV)

4. **In spite of all that God has done, there is still something *you* must do!**

Romans 10:9–13

9 That if thou shalt **confess with thy mouth the Lord Jesus**, and **shalt believe in thine heart that God hath raised him from the dead, thou shalt be saved**.
10 For with the heart man believeth unto righteousness; and with the mouth confession is made unto salvation.
11 For the scripture saith, Whosoever believeth on him shall not be ashamed.

12 For there is no difference between the Jew and the Greek: for the same Lord over all is rich unto all that call upon him.

13 For whosoever shall call upon the name of the Lord shall be saved.

(KJV)

After being saved you need to be baptized and unite with a Bible-centered Church for teaching and fellowship with other believers.

This journey is not always easy. You will experience some ups and some downs; some thrills of victories and some agonies of defeat; some good days, some sick days, etc. But in the end, you will be blessed to spend eternity with the Lord Jesus Christ, and as the Holy Spirit through Paul puts it:

1 Corinthians 2:9

9 But as it is written, Eye hath not seen, nor ear heard, neither have entered into the heart of man, the things which God hath prepared for them that love him.

(KJV)

The Grace of our Lord Jesus Christ be with you all. Amen.

About the Author

Carlton L. Burford was born in Memphis, Tennessee, to Alfred Burford Sr. and Clara Johnson in November 1955 and is currently married to his loving wife, Bernetta L. Burford. He has three lovely daughters (Tiffany, Tonya, and Toya) and three grandchildren (Shayne, Alijah, and Kaleb).

He attended college at General Motors Institute of Technology and graduated in July 1978 with a bachelor's degree in mechanical/electrical engineering.

In November 1978, Pastor Burford was called by God into the gospel ministry and attended Midwestern Baptist College in Pontiac, Michigan, and in 1999 received an honorary doctorate of divinity degree from the Great Commission Bible College and Theological

University in Bowling Green, Kentucky. He is currently the founder and pastor of the Inner Peace Baptist Church in Nashville, Tennessee.

Pastor Burford believes that the Bible is the Word of God and is fully inspired and without error in the original manuscripts. He believes that there is one living and true God eternally existing in three persons (The Father, The Son, and The Holy Spirit) and that Jesus Christ is God's only begotten Son who was conceived by the Holy Spirit through a virgin birth.

www.ingramcontent.com/pod-product-compliance
Lightning Source LLC
Chambersburg PA
CBHW071016120626
46546CB00003B/1107